ONLINE HELP SYSTEMS

Design and Implementation

HUMAN/COMPUTER INTERACTION

A Series of Monographs, Edited Volumes, and Texts

SERIES EDITOR

BEN SHNEIDERMAN

Directions in Human/Computer Interaction
Edited by Albert Badre and Ben Shneiderman

Online Communities:
A Case Study of the Office of the Future
Starr Roxanne Hiltz

Human Factors In Computer Systems
Edited by John Thomas and Michael Schneider

Human Factors and Interactive Computer Systems
Edited by Yannis Vassiliou

Advances in Human/Computer Interaction Vol. 1
Edited by H. Rex Hartson

Advances in Human Computer Interaction Vol. 2
Edited by H. Rex Hartson and Deborah Hix

Expert Systems: The User Interface
Edited by James A. Hendler

Online Helps: Design and Implementation
Greg Kearsley

Empirical Studies of Programmers
Edited by Elliot Soloway and Sitharama Iyengar

Empirical Studies of Programmers Vol. 2
Edited by Gary Olson, Elliot Soloway and Sylvia Sheppard

Human-Computer Interface Design Guidelines
C. Marlin Brown

In preparation:

Human Factors in Management Information Systems
Edited by Jane Carey

Socializing the Human/Computer Environment
Jerry Vaske and Charles Grantham

ONLINE HELP SYSTEMS

Design and Implementation

Greg Kearsley

Ablex Publishing Corporation
Norwood, New Jersey 07648

Printed in the United States of America

LIBRARY OF CONGRESS
Library of Congress Cataloging-in-Publication Data

Kearsley, Greg, 1951–
Online help systems : design and implementation / Greg Kearsley.
p. cm. — (Human computer interaction series)
Bibliography: p.
Includes index.
ISBN 0-89391-472-X
1. Question-answering systems. 2. On-line data processing.
I. Title. II. Series: Human/computer interaction (Norwood, N.J.)
QA76.9.Q4K43 1987
006.3—dc 19 88-10462

Ablex Publishing Corporation
355 Chestnut Street
Norwood, New Jersey 07648

Contents

Preface *ix*

1 **Introduction** *1*
Why help systems are needed 2
What is a help system? 3
Conceptual models of help 4
Design alternatives 6
Research issues 7
Implementation considerations 8
Relationship between helps, training, and documentation 9
Who this book is for 10
What the rest of the book covers 11

2 **Design Alternatives** *13*
Static versus dynamic helps 14
Multiple levels of help 17
Accessing help systems 18
User versus system-initiated helps 19
Screen formatting 20
Extensibility 23
Other considerations 24
Summary 26

3 **Examples of Help Systems** *27*
Helps for a command language (CROSSTALK) 28
Data Entry Fields (VM SCHEDULE) 29

Multiple-level helps (WORDSTAR) 30
Multiple help options (MCI MAIL) 31
Context-sensitive helps (LOTUS) 33
Prompting helps (SHERPA) 35
Helps in a programming environment (SYMBOLICS) 37
Guiding a database search (MELVYL) 40
Hypertext (GUIDE) 41
Summary 43

4 **Research on Helps** *45*
Experimental results 46
Cognitive psychology 49
Artificial intelligence 56
Summary 59

5 **Implementation** *61*
Analyzing user requirements 63
Specifications 64
Prototyping 65
Coding/writing 65
Tryouts 66
Quality control 67
Releases 68
Maintenance 69
Cost/benefit tradeoffs 69
Summary 72

6 **Guidelines** *73*
Make the help system easy to access and easy to return from 76
Make helps as specific as possible 76
Collect data to determine what helps are needed 78
Give users as much control of the help system as possible 79
Different types of users need different helps 80
Help messages must be accurate and complete 80
Don't use helps to compensate for poor interface design 82
Summary 83

7 **Summary & Conclusions** *85*
For DP/MIS managers 86
For software designers/developers 87

For training/documentation specialists 89
For researchers 90
For the rest of us 91

Glossary *93*

References *97*

Appendix A: Programming Considerations *101*

Appendix B: Software Tools *107*

Author Index *111*

Subject Index *113*

Preface

Help systems are a relatively recent development in the design of computer programs. Prior to about 1975, help capabilities were rare and found in only a small number of systems. Today, help capabilities are usually considered essential components of well-designed software. A program that lacks help features is rated as incomplete or inadequate.

Why have help capabilities become so important? The answer lies in the increasing expectations we have about usability. Over the past decade, a major shift occurred in the nature and scope of computer usage. Computer systems have become ubiquitous: automated banking, word processing, electronic mail, order processing, travel reservations, electronic check-outs in supermarkets and libraries, and, of course, home computers. Computers are now used daily by all types of individuals, ranging from 10-year-olds to corporate executives.

Today's computer user expects to be able to use a computer system with minimal or no training and with no special technical expertise. Yet the computer system and the transaction to be performed may be highly complex and sophisticated. The burden of designing a highly usable system rests with the software engineer. Help systems represent one of the primary components available to achieve the desired degree of usability.

Alas, the design of an effective help system turns out to be a very difficult task. When someone requests help, they normally want a specific explanation for an immediate problem. If the information provided is not specific enough, the help is not very helpful. Designing a help system that can provide exactly the right information desired requires a tremendous amount of effort.

Help systems are closely related to online documentation and training. In fact, the distinction between online help, documentation, and training is often fuzzy. When a user needs help, it is often difficult to classify the explanation provided as advice, information, or instruction. Because of this close relationship, developers of documentation and training should have a strong interest in help systems (and vice versa).

This book attempts to summarize our current knowledge about the design and implementation of help systems. It reviews the results of research on helps as well as examining examples of help systems in existing software. Guidelines for design and implementation are also provided.

It is hoped that this book will make the design of help systems a little easier and stimulate further research and experimentation on the topic.

Like any author, I am much in debt to many people who shared their ideas with me. I would in particular like to acknowledge the contributions made by John Carroll, Wendy Ebersberger, Wallace Judd, William Mosteller, H.M. Parsons, Ben Shneiderman, and Jan Walker. They helped make this a better book than it would have otherwise been.

Greg P. Kearsley

1

Introduction

Chapter 1 provides an overview of the major issues in the design and implementation of help systems. It also outlines the purpose and organization of the book.

Why Help Systems Are Needed

Theoretically, it is possible to design computer programs that are so well designed and tested that no user assistance is ever needed. It is also theoretically possible to design aircraft that never crash, buildings that can withstand earthquakes, and boats that are completely unsinkable.

Nonetheless, we don't count on such theoretical possibilities because our understanding of events and ability to predict outcomes is imperfect. In the case of computer programs, we cannot always anticipate what users will do or how programs will be used. Helps provide an insurance policy against less-than-perfect design.

Figure 1–1 lists some of the questions a user might have while using a program. Well-designed directions, screens, menus, and feedback messages should eliminate most of these questions but a help system is needed to deal with any that are not answered.

One of the reasons why it is so difficult to develop a program that works flawlessly for all users is that each user is different. People differ in terms of computer background or task experience, their assumptions and expectations about the way a program works, and dozens of personality characteristics such as reading speed, attention span, learning style, or patience. As a consequence of these factors, each individual reacts differently to a program. Because it is impossible to predict all of these varia-

- What can I do next?
- How should I respond?
- What does this mean?
- Where am I?
- How can I do this?
- What happened?
- How can I change this?
- Why didn't that work?

Figure 1–1. Examples of user questions

tions in user behavior, the best strategy is to build a "safety net" that catches people when they do something not anticipated in the system design. Helps are an important part of this safety net.

Helps contribute to the overall usability of a program by reducing the time it takes to complete an online transaction and the number of errors made. This improves user performance and satisfaction, both of which are important outcomes in terms of the marketability and acceptance of software. When the software is used for real-time financial, manufacturing, communications, or utility networks, improvements in usability may avert or minimize costly system failures. For programs used in medical/life support, weapons control, avionics, or emergency systems, increases in usability may have life or death consequences.

What Is a Help System?

A help system is one or more programs designed to provide user assistance embedded in a larger program or computer system. Although help programs are usually completely integrated with the application system they provide help with, they may also be separate and run concurrently with the system.

Help systems consist of two fundamental aspects: the interface and the content. The interface includes how the help messages are displayed, how the user accesses the help system, how the help system can be extended, and so on. The content is what the help messages say. Both aspects are equally important. If the help system is difficult to use because of poor interface design, it fails to be helpful. If the content of the help messages is unclear or inaccurate in some way, the help system also fails.

Help features may be built into existing components of the system. For example, the error-handling component of a system may be designed so that it tries to help the user determine what caused an error and what steps they can take to recover from the error. Similarly, help messages can be written for all of the major functions or operation in a system so that an explanation can be provided when a help request is made.

The design of a help system is closely tied to the design of the overall system. Help displays depend upon the display capabilities of the system, as do input methods, disk storage and access, printing, and so on. Although help systems do not necessarily have to work the same way as the system they support does, it is usually a desirable characteristic.

Conceptual Models of Help

A good way to introduce some of the major considerations in the design and implementation of help systems is to look at some conceptual models that illustrate the structure and function of help systems. These models are special cases of more general models of user behavior (e.g., Anderson, 1983; Card, Moran, & Newell, 1983; Shneiderman, 1987).

Figure 1–2 illustrates three major experience dimensions that users may differ on: task, computer, and program. The model suggests that users may be deficient in their skills or knowledge of the task, the computer system, or the specific program. Some common situations are the task expert who is thoroughly familiar with the job but has never used a computer or the program before; the computer whiz who is an expert computer user but does not know the task and has never used this specific program before, and the "technician" who knows how to use the program well but knows little about the task or computers.

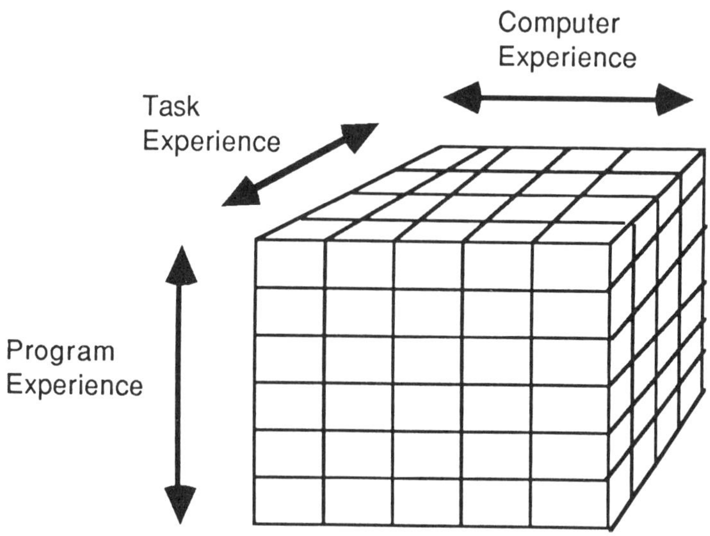

Figure 1–2. Three Major User Dimensions That Help Systems Should Address

Each of these types of users is likely to need slightly different types of help. For example, a user who is familiar with computers is likely to want different kinds of explanations about the program and have different types of problems than someone who has no computer experience. Furthermore, people change along each of these dimensions over time—so help systems need to extend across these three dimensions to match user changes.

Theoretically, a comprehensive help system would contain a response or message for every distinct user type or state represented in Figure 1–2. In practice, this is usually not possible. Instead, data is collected to discover which specific cells in the matrix correspond to typical user problems and the other cells are ignored.

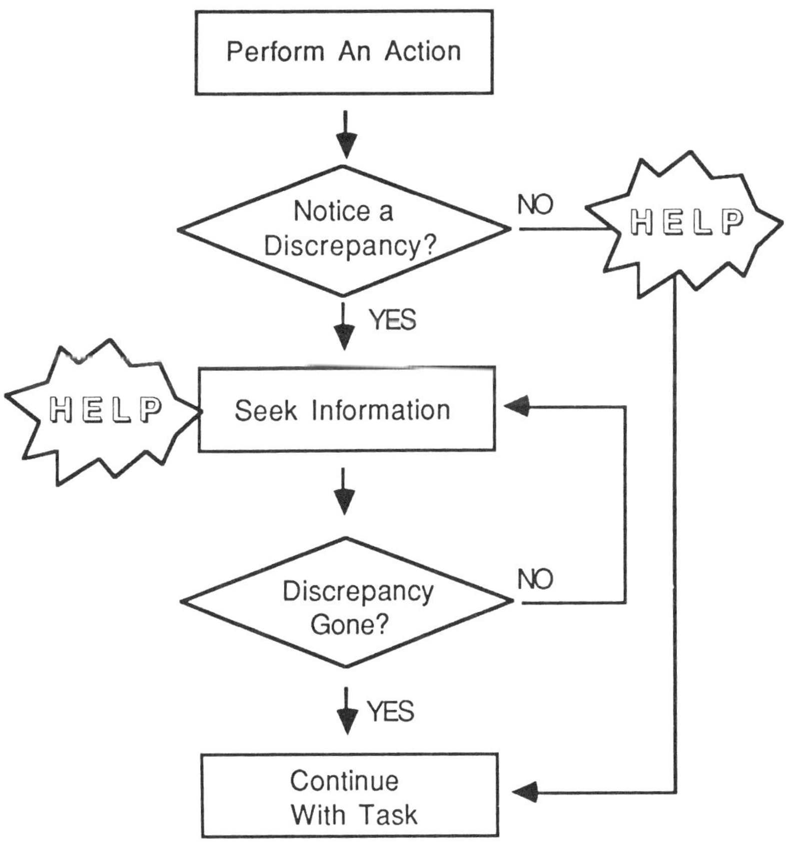

Figure 1–3. Process Model of Help System

Figure 1–3 shows another conceptual model of help systems—this one represents the process of requesting or receiving help information. This model suggests that a help request always follows some sort of discrepancy between what was expected and what actually occurred (recognized either by the user or the system). The user or system needs more information to determine what action to take to resolve the discrepancy. This is the point at which the user will request help or the system will provide it.

This model suggests that to build a comprehensive help system, every potential discrepancy between the user's expectations and actual program performance would need to be examined. Once again, in practice this is not normally possible and user data (or the experience of the program designers) is used to determine the most frequently occurring discrepancies.

Both of the models just discussed illustrate the point that the design of a help system could be an enormous undertaking. To keep the task manageable, we must focus on a smaller set of design issues and make use of any theoretical principles and practical guidelines available.

Design Alternatives

Designing an effective help system is a complex process. There are many alternatives to consider and many trade-off decisions to be made. For example, it is necessary to decide whether the help system will be static (like an online reference manual), context sensitive (make inferences about what advice to give or action to take), or dynamic (engage the user in a dialog). There is a significant difference in the kind of help information these three types of helps can provide and also a big difference in the design time required for each.

Other major design issues include what kind of help messages to provide (i.e., how many levels); how helps are accessed (control structures and activation); how the helps will be displayed (screen formatting); and how help messages will be modified (extensibility). There are also a host of minor issues such as which file structures to use; how helps will print; personalization (i.e., bookmarks); shared access through networks; and hardware/software constraints imposed by the computer system used.

Every software designer/developer (or his/her manager) will

need to make decisions about which alternatives are important for the application at hand. Knowledge of what design alternatives are possible is the first step in the design of effective help systems.

Research Issues

A major limitation to the current design of help systems is that it is largely trial and error. There is no validated theoretical framework that identifies what kinds of help are likely to be needed for a particular application. One of the reasons why there is a lack of useful theory for help systems is the absence of systematic research on the topic.

Experimental studies of help systems have investigated issues such as the following:

- Are different types of helps needed for experts and novices?
- What are the differences between user versus system-initiated help messages?
- What are the differences between online and offline helps?
- How can the effectiveness of helps be measured?

Although these studies and their results (discussed in Chapter 4) provide some general insights about the design of help systems, a great deal more research is needed to identify detailed principles.

Research in various areas of cognitive psychology and artificial intelligence hold promise for development of models that are useful in the design of help systems. Some of the issues that need to be addressed by such research are:

- Can domain/application independent help systems be developed?
- How large does a help system have to be in order to provide good advice?
- How can a help system recognize that the user has a problem?
- What are the best ways to model the user and represent user knowledge so a help system can make correct interfences about what help is needed?

- What kind of dialog (natural language, menu selections, command languages) works best for help systems?

In the absence of answers to questions such as these, designers must rely on guidelines derived from practice (see Chapter 6) and data collected during the implementation process.

Implementation Considerations

Although the implementation process for help systems is similar to the general software development cycle, some steps receive different emphasis. For one thing, the collection of data from user analysis and testing is critical to the development of effective help systems. This means that the prototype and tryout stages of development are very important for help system design. This is where the information needed to make final design decisions often comes from.

The actual coding stage may involve the use of different programming techniques or software tools. For example, a common requirement of help screens is to be able to overlay the application screens (i.e., "pop-up" windows). Another common requirement is that the help system reside in memory along with the application program. In some cases, it is desirable to develop the help system independently of the application program but still have it linked together.

Quality control is also a very critical step in the implementation of a help system. If there are inconsistencies or problems in the help system, the user will stop using it. Similarly, if help messages are not completely accurate and current, the usefulness of the help system evaporates quickly. The user must be able to trust the advice given by a help system; once the advice proves to be wrong or misleading, the credibility of the help system is destroyed.

To summarize, the implementation of a good help system is very dependent upon the collection of user data—during the initial specification process, during prototype design, and during quality control activities. Furthermore, different software tools may be needed for programming. Even software designers/developers with considerable experience may need to modify their methodology and approach in order to develop effective help systems.

Relationship between Helps, Training, and Documentation

A concern sometimes raised in the development of help systems is that the same information is already available in printed documentation or training materials/courses. Assuming for the moment that people use the documentation or have completed the training provided, it still does not serve the same function as a help system—which is to provide an *immediate* answer to a specific problem. In many cases, if the information is not immediately available, the user will try to guess, repeat a previous sequence, or ignore something not understood. This typically leads to further problems.

In reality, documentation often is not conveniently available and training was not completed or was very general in nature. So, the help system provides the only source of information and assistance available. Even when telephone hotlines or personal consultants are provided, they are likely to be used only for major problems and interrupt work flow significantly.

When people are using a computer program, they are interested in getting a particular task accomplished as quickly, and with as little effort, as possible. The task may be entering a customer's order, rerouting an aircraft, running a trial balance, sending an electronic mail message, or searching a database. When users run into a problem, they want an answer that involves minimal interruption from the task. A good help system addresses this need.

Online documentation and training also meet this criterion of immediate responsiveness. However, online documentation tends to be written and organized to provide descriptive information rather than specific assistance with a problem. Similarly, online training provides instruction, which is information written and organized to teach. For example, imagine someone who wants to use a text editor that is unfamiliar to them. They could ask for help about the specific operation currently being performed, they could ask for an explanation of how the editor works, or they could ask to be taught how to use the editor.

As this example illustrates, the distinction between online helps, documentation, and training is mostly a matter of intent. The information for all three could come from the same database but it may be presented differently to the user. Help information is focused on a specific problem; documentation attempts to explain something to the user, and training tries to facilitate learning. In practice, some online helps, documentation, and training sequences may be interchangeable. For this reason, no further distinction among the three types of online information is made in the rest of the book.

For some readers, the distinction (or lack of) between online helps, documentation, and training may have important organization or system design implications. Walker (in press) provides a survey of the issues and strategies in the design of online documentation and Brockman (1986) discusses the relationship between online and offline documentation. Judd (1986a) compares the nature of help versus training in more detail.

Who This Book is for

This book is written for software developers, including programmers, system analysts, computer scientists, and data-processing professionals. It is intended to be useful to both practitioners and researchers in terms of making everyday design decisions as well as identifying areas that need further study.

The book also is intended for technical writers and training specialists who may be involved in the design and development of online help, documentation, or training programs. Experience and skills in these areas should be brought to bear on the development of help systems.

The book should also be helpful to human factors engineers and psychologists in whose domain the design of help systems falls most directly. In fact, much of the existing research on help systems has been conducted by human factors scientists and cognitive psychologists.

Although the book does not require any formal background in the computer field, some familiarity with computers is assumed. A glossary of technical terms is provided at the end of the book.

This glossary should fill in the gaps for readers who have no computer background.

What the Rest of the Book Covers

The rest of the book consists of the following chapters:

Chapter 2. Design Alternatives. Discusses the alternative ways to design help systems including static versus dynamic helps, multiple levels, system versus user activation, screen formatting, control structures and other considerations.

Chapter 3. Examples of Help Systems. Examines a number of help systems in different programs as specific illustrations.

Chapter 4. Research on Help Systems. Reviews the results of past studies on helps as well as related research in areas such as artificial intelligence and cognitive psychology.

Chapter 5. Implementation. Discusses the many considerations in implementing helps, including cost/benefits, requirements analysis, prototyping, coding/writing, user tryouts, quality control, and maintenance.

Chapter 6 Guidelines. This chapter provides a concise set of guidelines for the design and implementation of help systems.

Chapter 7 Summary & Conclusions. The final chapter summarizes the major issues in the design and use of help systems from different perspectives.

The references provide further sources of information for readers who want to pursue specific topics in more detail.

There are four different ways that the subject of help systems can be studied: (a) in terms of the issues, (b) according to a developmental sequence, (c) in the context of what has been actually done, or (d) in terms of prescriptions. Chapters 2 and 3 provide a discussion of the design and research issues involved. Chapter 4 presents a variety of examples from commercially available software. Chapter 5 examines the development cycle. Chapters 6 and 7 provide guidelines and advice. Readers are encouraged to start with the chapters that most closely match their particular interest in the topic and peruse the other chapters later.

2

Design Alternatives

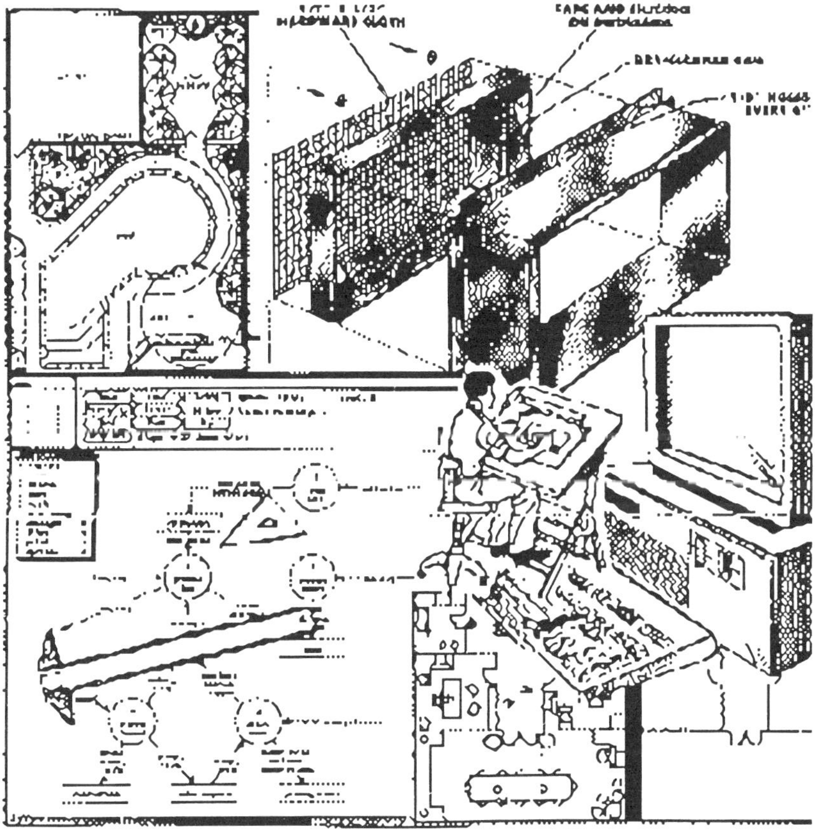

Chapter 2 discusses the different design alternatives for help systems, including static versus dynamic helps (context sensitivity), multiple levels, user versus system-initiated helps, screen formatting, control structures, and extensibility.

Examples of programs illustrating these design alternatives are provided in the Chapter 3. Appendix A discusses programming considerations associated with different design alternatives.

Static versus Dynamic Helps

The first major consideration in the design of a help system is whether the helps are static or dynamic. Static helps are independent of where the user is in the program and any previous user actions. On the other hand, dynamic helps will depend upon where the user is or previous actions (including help requests). Dynamic helps can be either context sensitive or dialogs. Context-sensitive help messages are determined by the current location or function being used. Dialog help messages are responses to user questions or answers.

Static helps are usually fixed text entries that serve as an online glossary. When help is requested, users are asked either to enter the term they want explained or to select a term from a list provided. In programs that use command languages, the helps are often explanations of individual commands. For example:

```
> HELP DIR
   The DIR command produces a list of all filenames in the current directory in order
   of creation date.  See also MKDIR, CHDIR, RMDIR, filename,pathnames.
```

As this example illustrates, it is common to include cross-references to related terms as part of the explanation.

In a static help system, requesting help without specifying a specific term normally produces a list of all terms available.

The simplest level of dynamic helps resembles static helps except that the program determines the appropriate help message to display based upon the last action of the user. For example:

```
>DIR
   lotus.exe       165340      9/10/82
   data1.wks         3778      2/20/87
   data2.wks         9450      2/24/87
>?
   The DIR command produces a list of all filenames in the current directory in order
   of creation date.  See also MKDIR, CHDIR, RMDIR, filename,pathnames
```

In this example, the user asked for help after typing a "DIR" command by typing a "?" The system responds with the explanation of the DIR command because it was the most recent user action performed.

This type of dynamic help is commonly used to provide explanations of error messages produced when a command is used incorrectly, for example:

```
>MKDIR
Missing Pathname
>?
   The MKDIR [pathname] command creates a new directory with the pathname
   specified. A pathname is one or more directory names, each separated by a
   backslash (\). Example: MKDIR \users creates a subdirectory named "users" in the
   current directory.
```

A more sophisticated form of dynamic help involves a different message for the same command at different points in the program. For example, if users ask for help about printing while they are creating a new record (e.g., a spreadsheet or database entry) they get a message pertaining to printing the record. However, if they ask for help about printing while editing files, the message explains the printing of files.

An even more elaborate type of dynamic help is one that is sensitive to a sequence of user requests or actions. A different help message may be produced for one sequence versus another. Consider the following sequence:

```
>help filename
   Filenames can be any name consisting of 1-8 characters.
>create data1/86
   Invalid filename
>help
   Valid characters in filenames are A Z, 0 9, $, &, %, @,-
   The following characters are invalid: !,/,\,{,},[,],(,),|,
>create data1-86 b:
   Incorrect drive designation
>help
   Drive designations (a:, b:, c:, etc.) precede the filename in a command.
   Example: create b:data1-86
>create b:data1-86
   File data1-86 created on b: drive
```

In this example, the first help message could be static, the second is triggered by the error message received, and the third uses the filename and drive designator provided by the user for the example provided in the message.

This example illustrates how increasing the degree of context sensitivity increases the usefulness of the help. The first message provides a general definition of a filename but omits details that were needed by the user. The next help message following the "Invalid filename" error focuses on the valid/invalid characters in a filename and is more helpful. The third help message explains exactly what the user needs to know to accomplish the file creation action desired. If the user could have phrased their help request in words at the beginning, it would have been something like, "How do I create a new file called data on the b: drive that has the date 1/86 in the name?"

This last point suggests that the most powerful form of help would be a dialog between the user and the system. The goal of the dialog is to allow the system to identify exactly what the user needs help with and then to provide this help. For example, consider the following help dialog for a user trying to perform a copy operation in a spreadsheet program (adapted from Judd, 1986b):

```
What do you want to copy?  (R)ow or (C)olumn
>C
Move the cursor to the top of the column you want to move.
> {cursor moved to cell A4}
OK. Now press the <end> and <down> keys.
> {end and down keys pressed}
Is this the last cell you want to copy?  (Y)es  (N)o
> N
Fine. Move the cursor to the last cell in the column you want to move
using the <down> key.
> {cursor moved to cell A23}
OK. Now move the cursor to the right of the cell you want to
move the column to and press Enter.
> {cursor moved to cell D4 and <Enter> pressed}
```

As this sequence illustrates, a dialog-type help guides the user through a problem, providing step-by-step instructions.

Developing a dialog-type help system requires a tremendous amount of time. Every response alternative in the dialog and possible user action must be checked and appropriate feedback provided. In the example above, it would be necessary to check that the user presses the correct keys and moves the cursor to valid locations.

The use of natural language for dialog-type help systems is discussed in Chapter 4.

Multiple Levels of Help

A second design alternative for helps is to provide multiple levels of explanation for successive help requests. Thus, the first help request produces a general explanation or definition and successive requests produce additional or more detailed information. For example:

```
>HELP DIR
   The DIR command produces a list of all filenames in the current directory in order
   of creation date.[More]  See also MKDIR, CHDIR, RMDIR, filename,pathnames.
>HELP
   The DIR command has the format: DIR [n:] [pathname].
  Specifying a drive designator or pathname will list  all files of the
  specified drive or directory. Files are listed with their size in bytes
  and the date of creation or last modification.  [More]

>HELP
  The DIR command has two parameters: DIR [n:] [pathname] [/P] [/W].
  The /P pauses after each full screen listing; the /W displays file names in
  columns across the screen without showing file size or creation date. [End]
```

In this example, successive requests produce more specific information about the format of the DIR command. The terms [More] and [End] are used to indicate whether additional information is available.

Instead of additional detail, subsequent requests could elicit examples, qualifications on use, or descriptions of related commands. In fact, helps can be linked together to form associative networks so that repeated help requests provide a path through the help file. The last level of each help is linked to an appropriate level in another help.

There are other ways to let users access multiple helps instead of successive requests. The user may specify the level of help desired by setting an option, for example, terse, detailed, with examples, with constraints, and so on. Alternatively, the user may specify the level of help desired in the request, for example, "?" versus "???" or "Help" versus "Help3." Different kinds of help can be specified by different help terms such as "Define", "Explain", "Example", or "Limitations".

Instead of specifying a level of help, the user may also be able request help on a specific parameter or option, for example,

>Help DIR /P
The /P parameter of the DIR command produces a pause after a full screen listing.
>Help filename -
The "-" is a valid filename character.
>Help print /laserjet
To print using the HP Laserjet, use PRINT PRN=HPLZR.

The capability to recognize help requests for specific parameters or options requires a more elaborate parser and more comprehensive help files than are needed to respond to successive requests for help of an unspecified nature. Not only must the help files contain more information, but more structure is required as well.

The choice of levels in a help system should be based upon typical user needs. For example, O'Malley et al. (1983) describe a proposal for a multilevel help system for UNIX, a popular operating system with hundreds of commands. They propose three levels: (a) quick reference, (b) task specific, and (c) full explanation. The quick-reference level is intended to provide a reminder of the correct syntax and options for each command. Task specific helps are focused on command lines, that is, commands and options used to perform a specific task such as printing, deleting, searching, and so on. Full explanations are descriptions of entire programs and system features that cut across specific commands. Each of these three levels is intended to meet a different type of user need: Level 1 serves as a memory aid, Level 2 explains how to perform new or unfamiliar tasks, and Level 3 is a tutorial about using UNIX.

Accessing Help Systems

There are three principal ways for users to activate helps: by typing a help command, by pressing a designated help key, or by selecting a help option from a program menu. Each has its advantages and disadvantages.

Typed input has the advantage that a complex syntax can be implemented allowing specification of multiple terms or levels. The disadvantages of typed input are that syntax errors may be made in the input, the user has to remember the syntax of help options (leading to a "help help"), and a parser will be needed for complex helps.

Help keys (e.g., using a function or control key) have the advantage that they can be activated easily and independently of typed input. A disadvantage of help keys is that they may be forgotten unless the user is reminded by a prompt that is constantly displayed on the screen (e.g., "F1=Help").

The major advantage of including help as a menu option is that it is visible and evident to users every time they look at the menu. Both help keys and help menu options require further specification of the help needed, (unless they are providing a context sensitive message), whereas typed input allows immediate specification. The additional specification usually involves the presentation of a list of help terms or help index that the user selects from.

These three access methods are not exclusive and can be combined. For example, pressing a help key could produce a prompt line asking the user to type in their help request. Many systems that use pull-down menus also provide control codes for each option as well. Thus, help may be activitated either by selecting help from the menu bar or by pressing the Control H or "?" key.

In addition to these three access methods presently in use, there is a fourth type of access possible in programs organized as "hypertext" (see Conklin, 1987). In a hypertext program, major terms or control options can be selected to produce a further elaboration, which may be text or graphic in nature, and which may also be elaborated. Applying the hypertext concept to helps, any major term or command in a program could provide help directly by being selected (see the GUIDE example in the next chapter). Hypertext is likely to become increasing popular in future software and is ideally suited to help systems.

User versus System-Initiated Helps

Up to this point in the chapter, we have assumed that the help request is initiated by the user. However, it is also possible to have the program determine when to present help messages and what messages to present.

System-initiated messages are presented to the user as advice or suggestions. They are usually triggered by error conditions or other evidence that the user has a problem (e.g., missing parameters, repetition of exactly the same command, a long lapse in response, out of range responses, etc.). For example, if the user enters an incorrect command, the system may respond by listing all the correct alternatives. The system may first ask the user if help is desired or simply present a help message.

Users often perceive system-initiated help messages as an interruption and prefer to initiate help requests. However, system-initiated help messages make sense for systems where incorrect user actions could result in serious consequences (e.g., nuclear power plants, aircraft controls, medical/life support). This is also true for destructive actions such as deletions, file replacements, or file renaming. Check messages (e.g., "Are you sure you want to delete this file? Y/N") are a common form of system-initiated help messages.

System-intiated help messages also make sense to help frequent users optimize their use of a system. Helps can point out shortcuts and unused features to the user. For example, the system may detect that a user continually uses a series of separate keystrokes or commands that can be replaced by a more global function or macro command. An optimization table can be created that looks for examples of ineffective usage or underutilization and suggests improvements.

If system-intiated help messages are used, it is recommended that the user be given the option of turning them off or specifying the level of message enabled (e.g., advisory, caution, warning). Note that it is possible to have a combination of user and system-initiated help messages. Messages of a certain priority are automatically displayed, whereas lower priority messages are only displayed when help is requested.

Screen Formatting

Display of the help message is another important design consideration. There are two primary considerations in formatting help displays: (a) location and size of the message area, and (b) scrolling or paging within the message area. Figure 2–1 illustrates the various design alternatives for location of help messages.

To a large extent, the possible formatting options are a function of the screen management capabilities of the operating system and graphics display capabilities of the hardware involved. Operating systems and hardware which support bit-mapped graphics

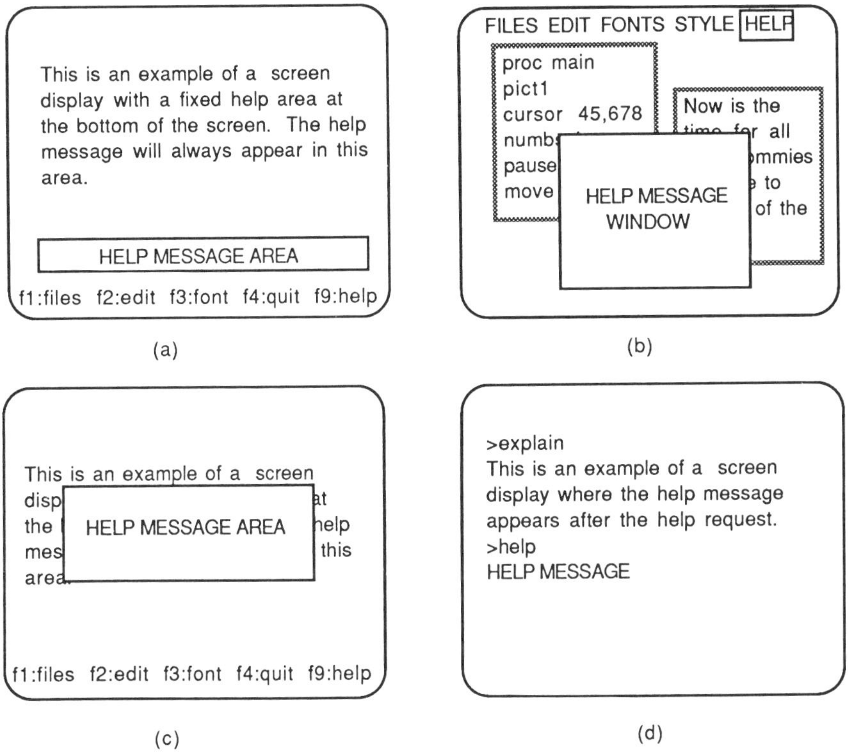

Figure 2–1. Examples of Help Screen Formatting: (a) Fixed Message Area at Bottom of Screen, (b) Movable Overlapping Window, (c) Fixed Overlapping Window, and (d) Command Line

allow independent *windows* that can be overlapped and positioned anywhere on the screen. In some systems, the default location and size of windows are set by the program but, after initial display, they can be moved and resized by the user. In other systems, windows overlap the current display but cannot be moved or resized.

In systems without windowing capability, the help message may be displayed in a fixed area at the bottom of the screen (often the bottom two lines of the screen are reserved for help and error messages), or the help area may use a full screen that replaces the current application screen when help is selected. In programs that use commands or dialog-type help systems, the help message may appear on the next available line.

Display of helps messages in windows is to be preferred over full-screen or scrolling-type formats. Full-screen display and scrolling create memory problems for users because they have to remember the details of the help request. With a window, they can simultaneously see both the application context and the help information.

The other formatting consideration for help messages is whether the message should page or scroll if its length exceeds the space available in the window or message area. In some windowing systems, a scroll-bar capability is provided that lets the user move the message up and down in the window as desired (see Figure 2–2). The same effect can be achieved using arrow or page up/page down keys.

In other windowing systems, the help message is arranged as a series of separate pages that the user can move through by using specified keys (see Figure 2–3).

However the help is displayed, it is critical that the user be able to return to the application with a single keystroke (i.e., pressing a designated key or clicking the mouse). This ensures that the help request will be a minimal interruption of work flow.

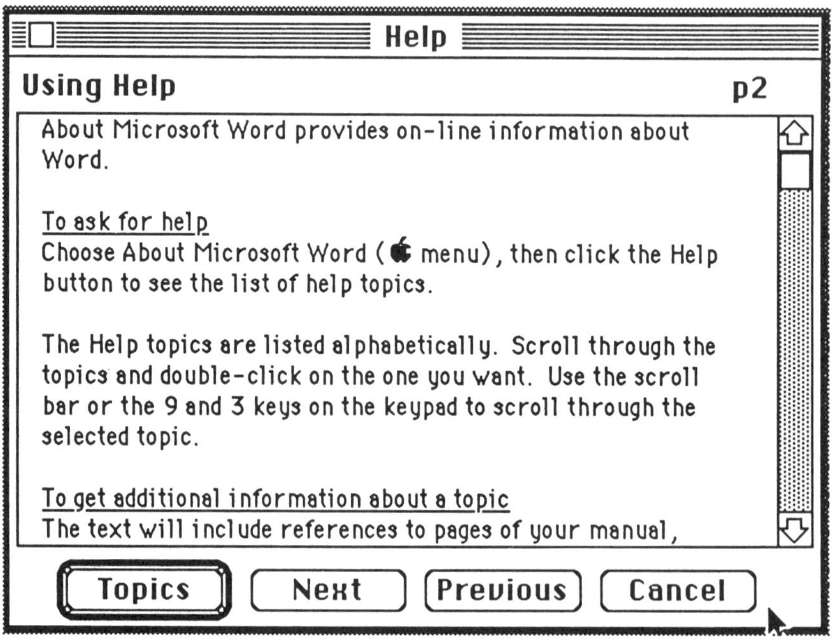

Figure 2–2. Example of Help Window with Scroll Bar

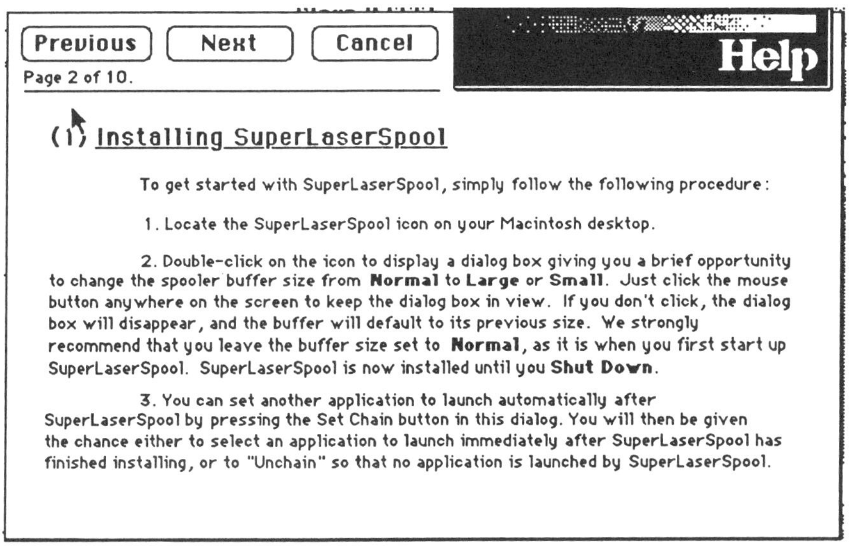

Figure 2–3. Example of Fixed Help Window That Uses Paging

Extensibility

In designing a help system, it is important to provide capability for the user to add or modify the help messages. For example, the user might want to add information to a help message to reflect the way a command is used for a particular application. Alternatively, the content of a help message may need to be changed for a particular configuration of computer system.

In addition to the modification of help messages, it should also be possible for a user to specify multiple access paths. For example, it should be possible to define synonyms or multiple contexts for any particular help message. This allows the help system to be adapted to idiosyncratic usage.

Allowing users to modify help messages does raise an issue of program integrity: What happens if a user changes a help message so that it gives incorrect or misleading advice? If this is a multiuser system with a shared database, the incorrect message may affect many users. The best solution to this dilemma seems to be to allow users to add to, but not modify, the original content of help messages.

Designing a help system that is extensible has a number of programming implications. For example, if the user can define synonyms or rename helps, it is desirable to maintain a single directory that the program checks before executing a help message. If the user can modify only a portion of the help message, a protection scheme must be written that prevents change to the fixed part. In a multiuser system, users must be given their own file space where changes to the master copy of helps are stored. Although these are implementation rather than design concerns, the designer should be aware that extensibility presents programming challenges, especially if the help system is being retrofitted to an existing application program. (See Appendix A for further programming considerations.)

It is worth noting that the same type of capabilites provided for user modification of helps will also be needed by the developers as well to create and maintain the help system. Thus, such capabilities should be designed into the help system from the beginning to assist developers.

Other Considerations

In addition to these major design issues, there a number of minor considerations including file structures, printing, bookmarks, networking, and hardware/software constraints.

Once the help system has been designed, a particular file structure for the help messages will need to be defined. The two primary alternatives are a single file with a unique code separating each message or as separate files for each help message. The first alternative may result in more efficient processing, whereas the second alternative may make development easier. In either case, it is desirable to store help messages as unformatted text (ASCII) files so that they can be created and modified using any text editor/word processing program. However, this means that a formatting capability will need to be built into the help program so that messages are displayed correctly.

In many cases, users will want to print out help information to study it further or for future reference. This means that a screen print option needs to be available while help messages are displayed. Alternatively, a print capability should be provided as part of the help system so that users can print whatever messages they wish. Print capability is especially important when helps are being used as online documentation.

Bookmarking allows users to tag (and possibly name) specific help messages for easy referral later. This is especially useful in a large help system that consists of many topics and screens. To tag a message, the user selects a bookmark option while viewing the message. When selecting help, the user has an option to see all, or just the bookmarked, messages. A bookmarking capability allows users to customize the help system to their own needs and filter out information that is not of interest.

In a networked (i.e., multiuser) system, it is possible to provide facilities for users to help each other (see Bannon, 1986). This includes bulletin boards, electronic mail, and real-time messaging. Bulletin boards can be used to broadcast recent changes or problems with the system to all users. Alternatively, bulletin boards can be used to address specific problems, becoming an online diagnostic clinic. Similarly, electronic mail and real-time messaging with experienced users or consultants can serve the same purpose. In many cases, this kind of information can provide a dynamic and evolving help network. However, help systems built out of electronic message databases do not usually have the comprehensive and systematic structure of a built-in help system.

Finally, the particular nature of the software and hardware used places constraints on what kind of help system is possible. The significance of bit-mapped graphics capability was already mentioned in the discussion of screen formatting. Display capabilities will also affect the use of color and different fonts. The amount of memory (RAM) and disk space available affects the size of the help system. Help systems with hundreds of topics or messages can require a large amount of memory or disk space,—something to be taken into account in the initial design of the application and help system. The speed of the processor or system response time is also a consideration. If response time is poor, users will be discouraged from using the help system.

A common problem in large-scale systems is that a variety of different terminals will be used with different screen display, memory, and keyboard capabilities. In this case, help systems must be designed that can run on all terminals, or a terminal handling program needs to be designed that can automatically adjust the help system to the capabilities of different terminals.

Summary

When designing a help system, there are six major design decisions to be made:

- Static versus dynamic helps
- Number of levels of helps and their differentiation
- Access structures (typed vs. keys vs. menu option)
- System versus user initiation
- Screen formatting of messages
- Extensibility of helps

Other considerations include: file structures, printing, bookmarking, networking, and hardware/software constraints.

The choice of specific design alternatives is based upon the cost/benefit tradeoffs of development time versus increased usability.

Examples of different types of helps illustrating alternative designs are examined in Chapter 3. Cost/benefit tradeoffs are discussed further in Chapter 5.

3

Examples of Help Systems

Chapter 3 examines a number of actual help systems from commercially available software. These programs are used because they are representative of the current state of the art in software design. Each example illustrates a particular kind of help or design alternative.

Helps for a Command Language (CROSSTALK)

Many programs use a command language interface. A major function of the help system in such programs is to explain the syntax and action of the commands. The CROSSTALK communications program (marketed by Crosstalk Communications) illustrates this type of help. Figure 3–1 shows a sequence of three help requests in CROSSTALK.

The first request ("help" with no option) produces a list of all program commands. The second help request ("help help") results in an explanation of the help command. The third help request ("help load") generates an explanation of the load command.

```
 Command ? help

Valid commands :

LOad     MOde     QUit     WIdth    XDos     ATten    BLock    BYe
CApture  COmmand  DAta     DEbug    DIr      DUplex   FLow     HElp
F1       F2       F3       F4       F?       FIlter   LFauto   LIst
MEm      NAme     NO       NUmber   PArity   PRinter  RCve     REad
RQest    SAve     SCreen   SPeed    STop     TAbex    TIme     TYpe
UConly   WAit     WRite    XMit

 Command ? help help
Syntax  : Help (option)
Options : any valid CROSSTALK command
Displays "HELP" information. "Help"<CR> with  no option displays
a  list of all of CROSSTALK's commands.  If you need help with  a
command,  type "HELP XX" <CR>, where "XX" is the command you need
help with.  This command requires that the file "XTALK.HLP" be on
the  currently logged-in disk drive.  If the file is not present,
an  error  message  will be displayed.

 Command ? help load
Syntax: LOad (filename.typ)
Loads  and  executes CROSSTALK command files.  Command files  are
disk files containing commands for CROSSTALK to perform.
```

Figure 3–1. Example of Help Messages in CROSSTALK

This type of help is useful for users who want a quick reminder of the correct syntax or function of a command. It is also easy to design and implement. However, it does not provide any examples that would explain correct/incorrect use of a command; neither does it compare/contrast the functions of different and related commands nor provide explanations of important concepts that need to be understood to use the commands.

Data Entry Fields (VM SCHEDULE)

VM SCHEDULE is a system utility program developed by VM Software Inc. for users of the IBM VM operating system. Like

```
    Release 4.0            VMSCHEDULE        (c) 1987 VM Software Inc.

======================= Help Informastion ============================
                         REQUEST NAME

    The request name is a unique identifier for a request and all of
    its associated parameters. It is assigned when a request is first
    scheduled or copied. Names can be reused after a request is complete
    or cancelled.

    Names can be up to eight characters long (any characters can be used).
    To allow VMSCHEDULE to punch files, use only characters that are legal
    for CMS filenames. To QUERY requests, an asterisk (*) can be used for
    pattern matching, where a trailing asterisk indicates all requests
    with names matching the characters preceding the asterisk should be
    found.

    All request names currently known to VMSCHEDULE can be viewed using
    the QUERY subcommand, using an asterisk in the request name field.

    Request names can be altered from any of the multi-screen displays
    used for EXEC and SCHEDULE.

===>
         1=         2=        3= Quit  4=        5=        6=
         7= Backward 8 Forward 9=      10= Print 11=       12=
175I  Press PF3 or enter 'Quit' to return to previous screen.
```

Figure 3–2. Requesting Help in a Data Entry Screen (courtesy VM Software, Inc.)

many programs, VM SCHEDULE screens include data entry fields (see Figure 3–2). Since users often do not know what response is expected for a particular field (or have forgotten), help messages that provide an explanation of each field are often useful.

Figure 3–3 shows the help screen produced by pressing the PF1 key while the cursor is positioned at the "Request name" field. The user presses PF3 or types "quit" to return to the data entry screen.

Multiple Level Helps (WORDSTAR)

Wordstar (developed by MicroPro Corporation) is a widely used word processing program for PCs. It was one of the first programs to use a multilevel help system that users could adjust to their needs. User control of the program is via one and two-

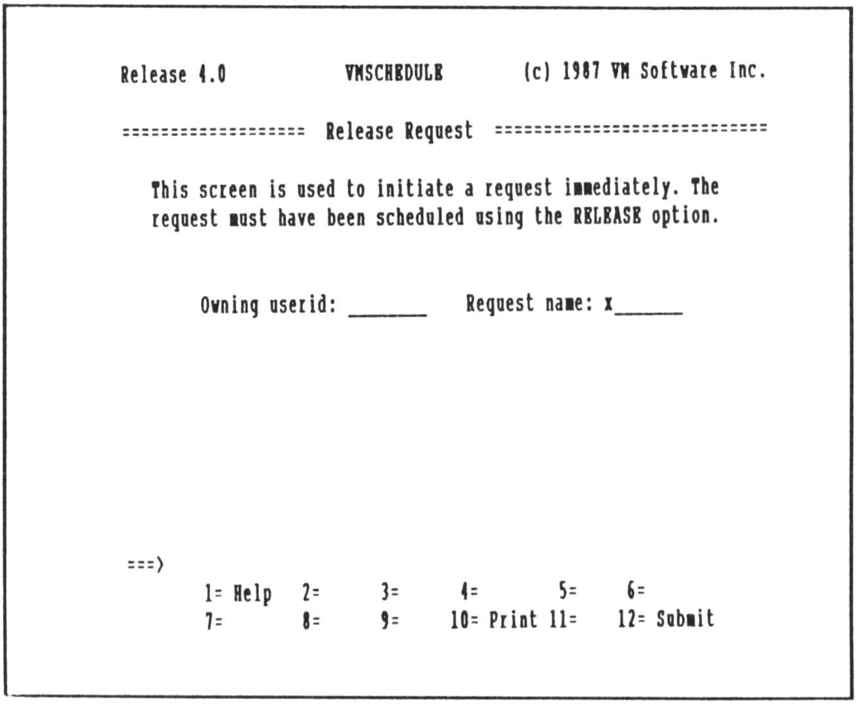

Figure 3–3. Help Screen for REQUEST NAME Field (courtesy VM Software, Inc.)

```
HELP LEVELS
  3 all menus and explanations displayed
  2 main editing menu (1-control-char commands) suppressed
  1 prefix menus (2-character commands) also suppressed
  0 command explanations (including this) also suppressed

CURRENT HELP LEVEL IS 3

ENTER Space OR NEW HELP LEVEL (0, 1, 2, OR 3):
```

Figure 3–4. The Four Levels of Help in WORDSTAR

character commands. Helps in the program consist of menus displayed at the top of the screen that define the commands.

The obvious benefit of these different levels is that it allows users to start with full menus and prompting messages while novices but turn off the helps as they become experienced. It also provides an easy way for someone to get reacquainted with a program they have not used for a while.

The program features four levels of help: (a) all menus displayed continuously, (b) the main menu suppressed, (c) prefix menus also suppressed, and (d) all prompting messages suppressed. Figure 3–4 shows the menu used to select the level of help desired.

Multiple Help Options (MCI MAIL)

MCI Mail is an electronic mail service. Like most of all online networks, it has a command language interface. The help system in MCI Mail offers a number of options including a help message that is sensitive to the current activity, a glossary, an index, a guide to printed documentation, and (if all else fails), a telephone hotline (see Figure 3–5).

While the MCI Mail help system is subject to the same limitations as mentioned earlier for the CROSSTALK program, it provides the user with a wider choice of help options. The limited context sensitivity also focuses the help message.

```
Command (or MENU or EXIT): help

-----------------------------------------------------------
|                    Command: HELP
-----------------------------------------------------------
|
|                 Welcome to MCI Mail!
|
| This menu is called the MAIN MENU. You may return to it
| by typing MENU at any prompt. The following is a description
| of the commands that you may use at the Main Menu.
|
| SCAN          Summarize the messages in your mailbox
|
| READ          Display messages with pauses between
|               messages and page breaks
|
| PRINT         Display messages without pauses between
|               messages and page breaks
|
| CREATE        Creates a message, including the envelope
|               and text
|
| Type HELP MAILBOX for information on your MCI Mailbox.
|
| Type HELP GLOSSARY for a reference guide to the MCI
| Mail commands.
|
| Type HELP INDEX for a complete listing of all topics that
| are available to you.
|
| Type HELP REQUEST for information on MCI Mail manuals
| and reference guides.
|
| Help is available to you at any prompt. When you're not
| sure what to do next just type HELP and an explanation
| will appear.
|
| If you need further assistance, call Customer Support
| at 1-800-424-6677 or send message TO: MCI HELP.
|
---------------- End of Help ------------------------------
```

Figure 3–5. Help Screen from MCI Mail

Context-Sensitive Helps (LOTUS)

Lotus 1–2–3 (from Lotus Development Corporation) is one of the most popular spreadsheet programs available for PCs. It features a context-sensitivity help system that provides help information relevant to the user's present location in the program (as determined by current menu selection).

Figure 3–6 shows the help screen that results from pressing the help key (F1) after having selected the "graph" option of the main menu. After viewing this help screen, the user can return to the spreadsheet by pressing the escape (ESC) key.

If the user then selected the "type suboption of the "graph"

```
A1:                                                                  HELP
Type  X  A  B  C  D  E  F  Reset  View  Save  Options  Name  Quit
Set graph type
---------------------------------------------------------- 229 -------
Graph commands -- Enter graph specifications; view a graph

- Select a graph setting or graph operation from the menu.
           (1-2-3 returns to this menu or to a submenu until you select Quit)

Graph settings are stored in worksheet files created with File Save and File
Xtract.  Graph Reset Graph cancels all graph settings.

In Ready mode, pressing {F10/Graph} draws a graph according to the current
settings.  At this Graph menu, select View to draw a graph.

Graph Settings           Graph Operations
--------------           --------------------------------------
Type                     Save     Create a graph (picture) file
X-range                  Name     Assign name to current settings
A-F ranges               View     Draw graph with current settings
Options                  Quit     Return to Ready mode
Reset
---------------------------------------------------------------------
Help Index
```

Figure 3–6. Help Message for "Graph" Option in LOTUS 1–2–3

command and pressed the F1 key again for help, they would see the screen depicted in Figure 3–7. This help message is specific to the suboption just selected.

Selecting help from the top-level menu of the program (i.e., before any options have been selected) produces the help index (see Figure 3–8). Each entry in the index can be selected for more detailed explanations.

For example, Figure 3–9 shows the result of selecting the topic "Special Keys" from the main index. Note that the detailed explanation displays related topics at the bottom of the screen. Thus, items in the LOTUS 1–2–3 help database are hierarchically organized and cross-referenced.

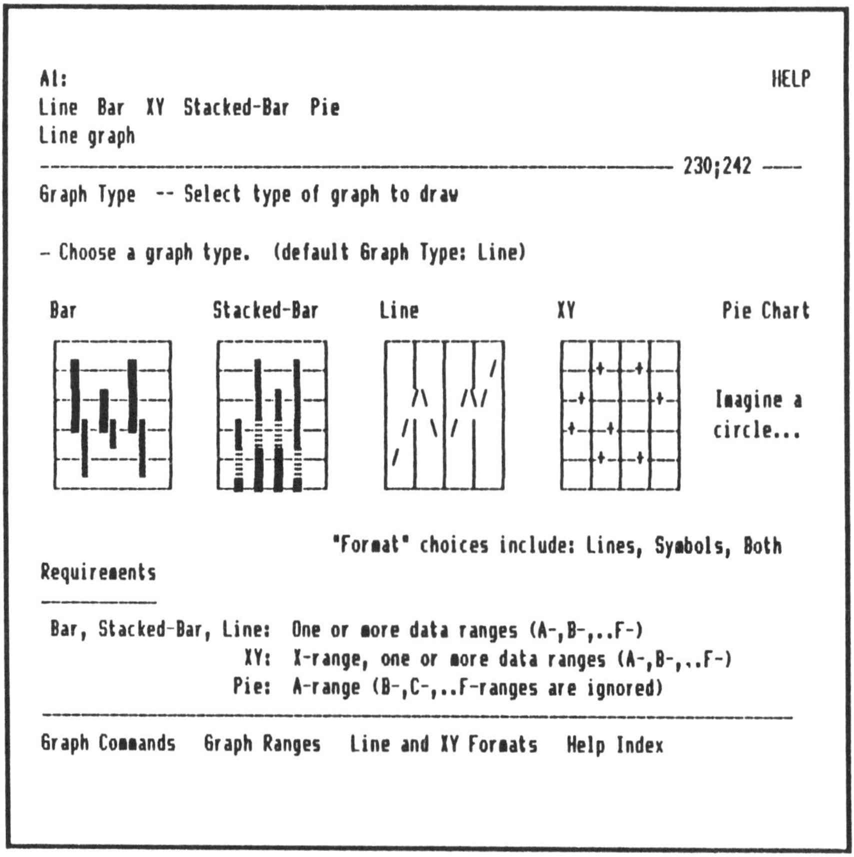

Figure 3–7. Help Message for "Type" Suboption in LOTUS 1–2–3

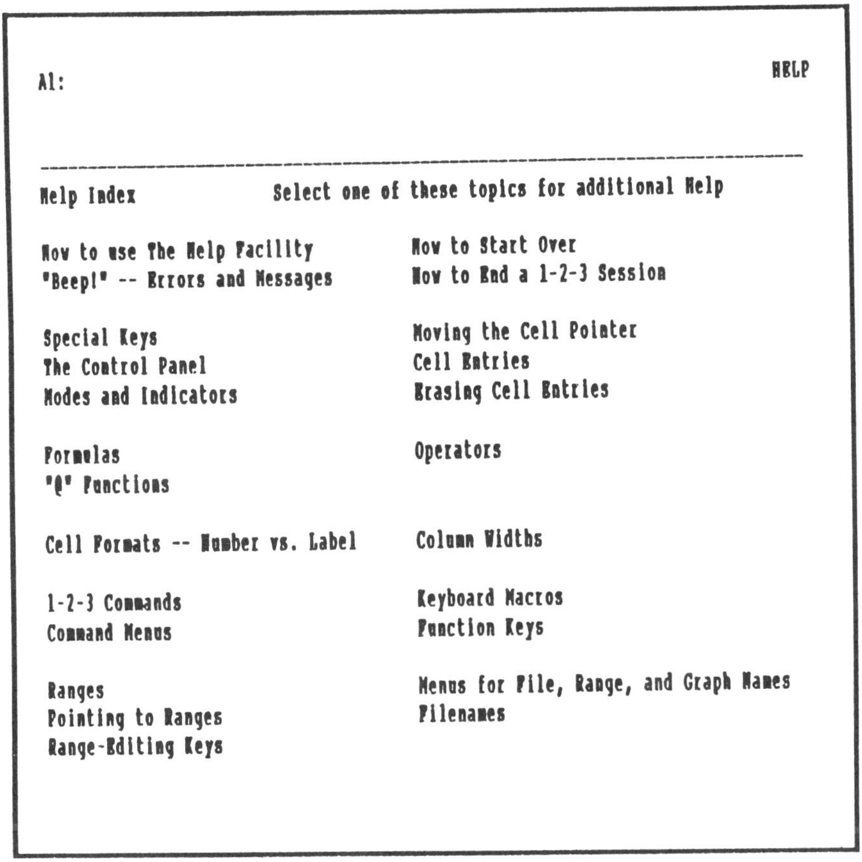

A1: HELP

Help Index Select one of these topics for additional Help

How to use The Help Facility
"Beep!" -- Errors and Messages

How to Start Over
How to End a 1-2-3 Session

Special Keys
The Control Panel
Modes and Indicators

Moving the Cell Pointer
Cell Entries
Erasing Cell Entries

Formulas
"@" Functions

Operators

Cell Formats -- Number vs. Label

Column Widths

1-2-3 Commands
Command Menus

Keyboard Macros
Function Keys

Ranges
Pointing to Ranges
Range-Editing Keys

Menus for File, Range, and Graph Names
Filenames

Figure 3–8. Help Index in LOTUS 1–2–3

The help system of LOTUS demonstrates how dynamic helps (achieved through context sensitivity and hierarchical organization of help items) can provide relatively specific information to the user. However, people often report becoming frustrated with the LOTUS help system because it is still necessary to read a lot of information to find an answer to a particular problem or question.

Prompting Helps (SHERPA)

SHERPA is a help program for LOTUS 1–2–3 developed by Com-Train that supplements and extends the help system provided

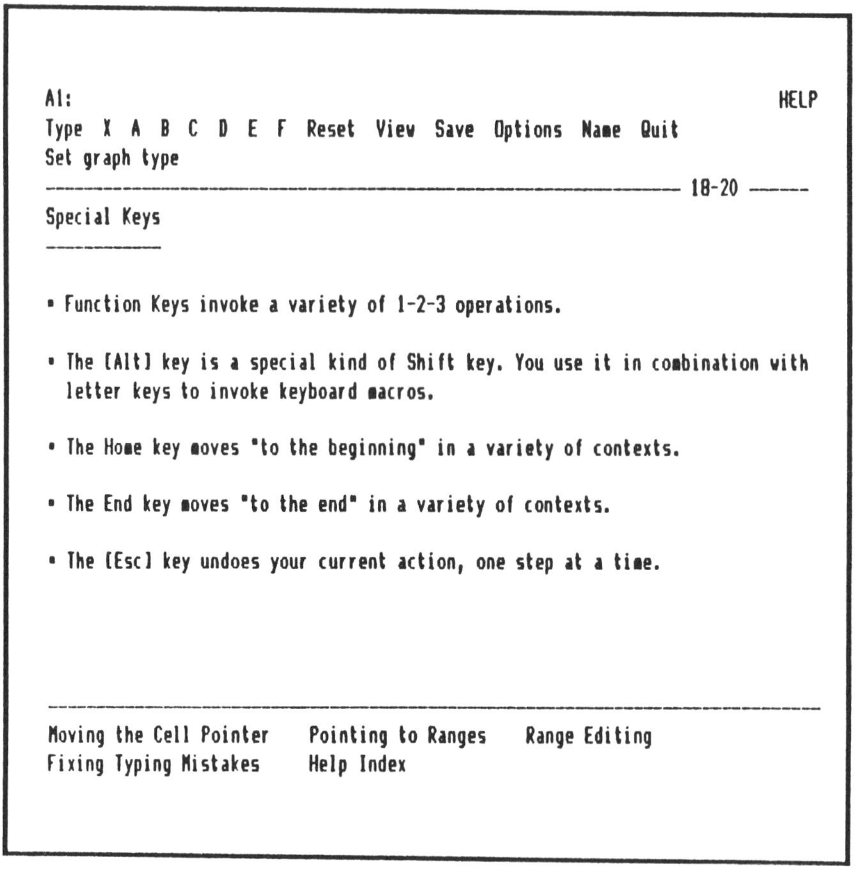

Figure 3–9. Help Message for "Special Keys" Topic in LOTUS 1–2–3

with LOTUS. The distinctive feature of SHERPA is that it can lead the user through the use of a LOTUS function step by step via a series of prompting messages.

Figure 3–10 illustrates the prompting capability of SHERPA. The user has asked for help with the topic of functions, specifically the use of the @AVG function. SHERPA prompts users through the use of the function in their actual application, providing corrective advice if the user makes a mistake.

SHERPA provides a good example of a dialog-type help system and one that combines both user and system-activated helps.

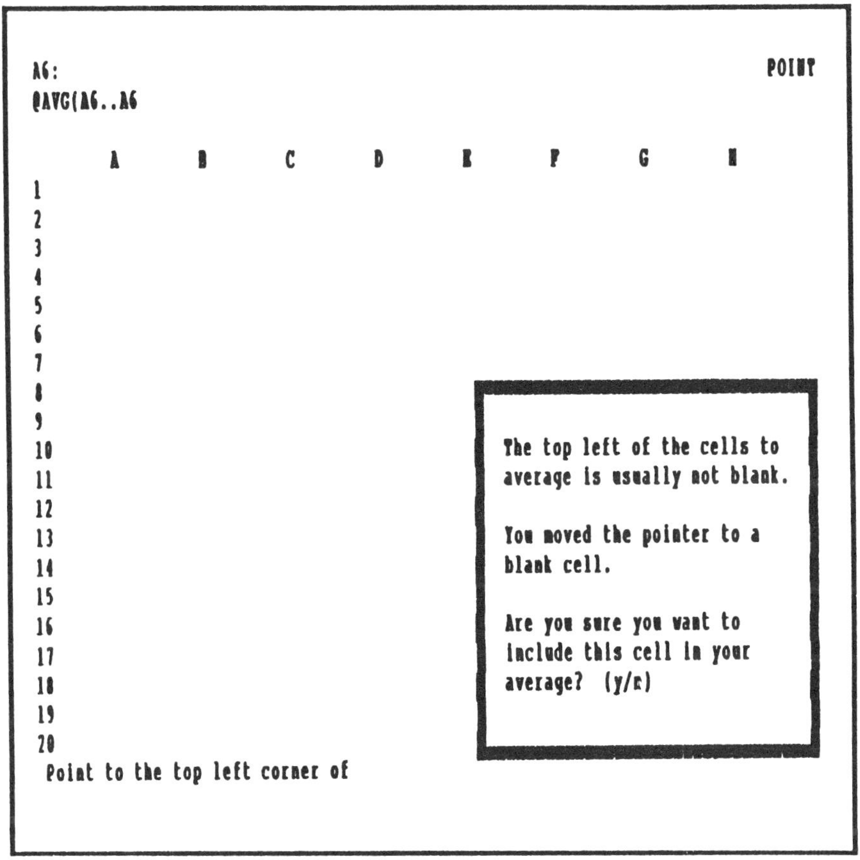

Figure 3–10. SHERPA Help Message for "AVG" Function

Helps in a Programming Environment (SYMBOLICS)

Expert computer users (such as programmers) also need help systems. This example describes some of the types of helps that are available for the LISP environment on Symbolics workstations.

Figure 3–11 shows an editor screen (Zmacs) in which the user has selected a particular function name ("SHOW-BITMAP") with the mouse and asked for an identification of the current arguments for this function via a key press. The list of arguments appears in the message window at the bottom of the screen. Note

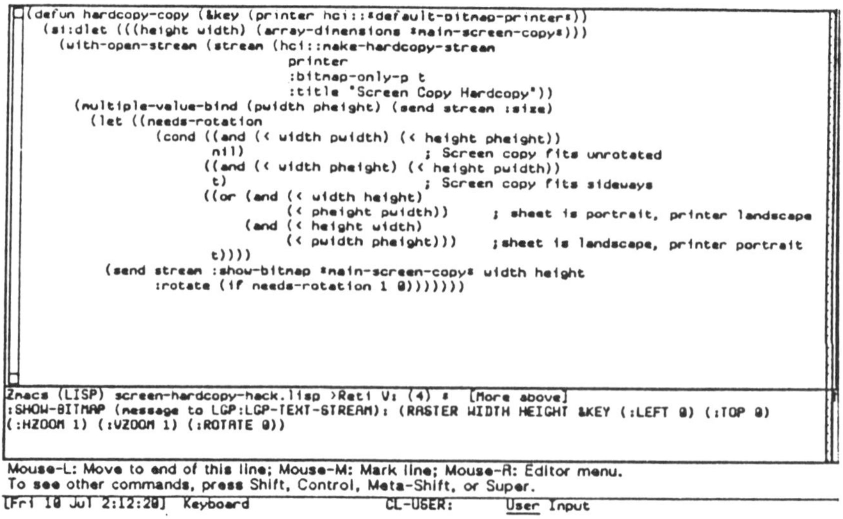

Figure 3–11. Getting Information About Program Arguments (courtesy Symbolics, Inc.)

that this information comes from the function itself, so it is always correct.

Figure 3–12 shows another type of help—accessing the online documentation for the system. The user has selected a particular function ("with-open-stream") with the mouse and asked for the documentation on that function via a key press. The documentation is displayed in a message window at the top of the screen. Note that there is a cross-reference to the general topic ("file-opening options") that the user could select if desired.

Figure 3–13 shows a help capability in a debugging program. In the example, the user has asked to list a directory which does not exist. The error-handling routine explains the problem and then lists the possible options (the default option is boxed).

Notice the help message at the bottom of Figures 3–11, 3–12, and 3–13. The actions of the mouse buttons mean different things at different places in the program. The help message indicates the current function of the three buttons (Left, Middle, Right).

As these examples illustrate, help systems can provide sophisticated assistance to advanced, as well as novice, users.

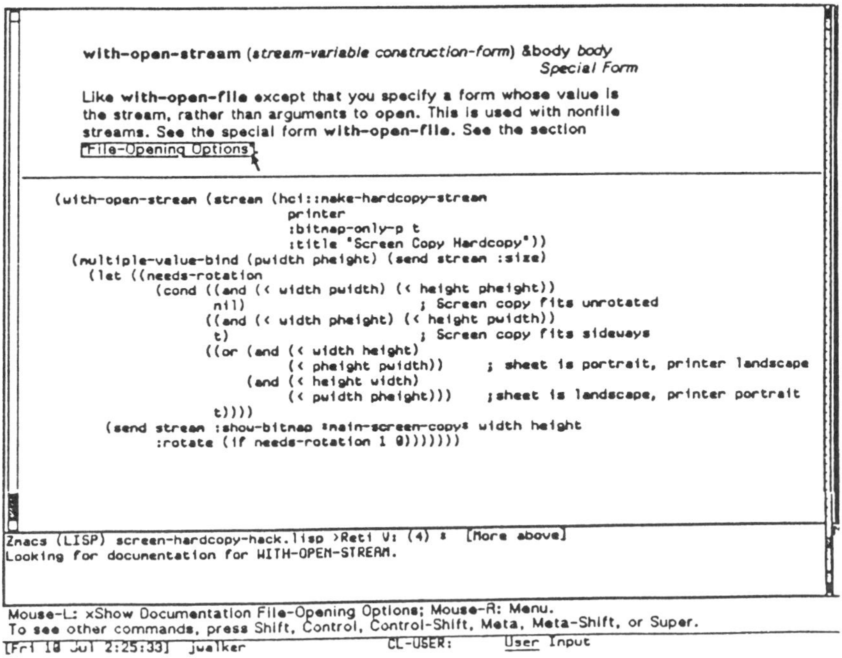

Figure 3–12. Accessing Program Documentation (courtesy Symbolics, Inc.)

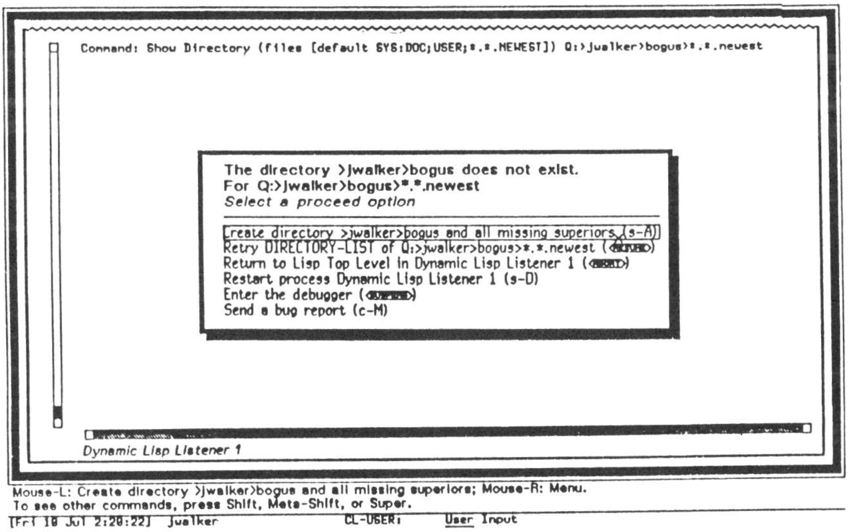

Figure 3–13. Help After an Error (courtesy Symbolics, Inc.)

Guiding a Database Search (MELVYL)

MELVYL is the online bibliographic catalog for the University of California library system. MELVYL is used every day by thousands of university staff and students in campus libraries, most of whom have no computer or database searching experience.

Figures 3–14 and 3–15 show the type of help provided when a user has trouble with a search command. As the figures show, the helps attempt to guide the user from the current step to the next. In Figure 3–14, the system explains what is missing in the FIND command.

In Figure 3–15, the help message provides suggestions about

```
-> find
Your FIND command does not contain a searchable index name.
Please type HELP for a list of indexes you can use.

- > help

A basic search request consists of three parts in the following order:
      FIND (index)  (keywords or exact key)

The part that is missing from your command is the index name.  Please be sure
that all three parts are included when you retype your command.


The indexes that can be specified in a FIND command are:

                        Keyword Indexes

To books:                                                To Periodicals:
  PA  Personal Author   TW  Title Word     SU  Subject   PE  Periodicals
  CA  Corporate Author  UT  Uniform Title SE  Series
  AU  Author  (PA  +  CA)

For more information, type EXPLAIN (or EXP) INDEXES or EXP followed by an
index name, e.g. E XT.
```

Figure 3–14. A Help Message in the MELVYL System That Explains What Is Wrong With a Command

```
-> find au=searyek
Search request: FIND AU=SEARYEK
Search result: 0 records at all libraries
Please type HELP for information on zero search results.

-> help
Your author search request
    FIND AU=SEARYEK
did not result in any retrievals at all libraries.
Suggestions:
*  Check your search request for typing errors.
*  Try alternate spellings, e.g., Newman/Neumann, McDonald/MacDonald.
*  If you have included a title with your author search, be sure it is
   preceded by the phrase AND TITLE WORD.
The item you want may be in your library even though you were unable to
locate it through the MELVYL catalog.  Please check your local catalog or
consult a reference librarian.
You can now:                                For more information, type:
   Begin a new search.                         EXPLAIN FIND.
   Begin a browse.                             EXPLAIN BROWSE.
   Use any other command.                      EXPLAIN COMMANDS.
   Type END to end your session.
```

Figure 3–15. Help Message in MELVYL System Provides Suggestions About Why Search Did Not Work

why the search did not work. Although this is not as helpful as a dialog system, it does provide quite a high degree of specific advice.

Hypertext (GUIDE)

GUIDE is a program for personal computers developed by OWL International that allows you to create and distribute hypertext documents. Different types of actions can occur when a user selects a marked object (i.e., a word, box, graphic): (a) another document is opened that elaborates on the object, (b) a temporary "note" window is displayed that provides elaboration only as

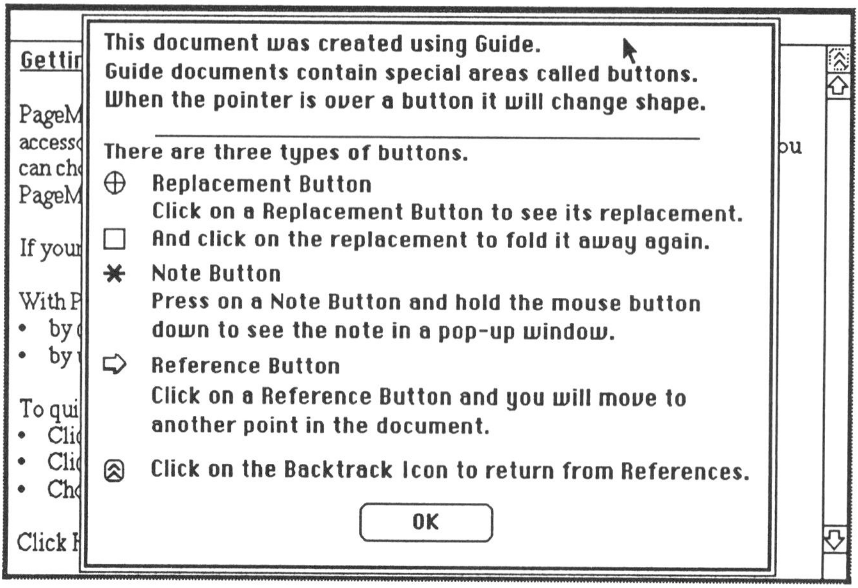

Figure 3–16. Guide Options in PageMaker Program

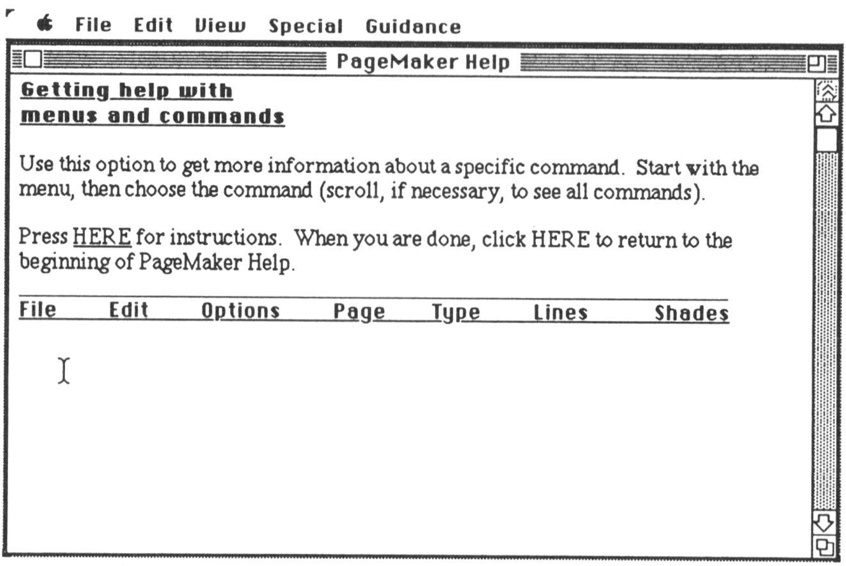

Figure 3–17. Example of Help Screen Using GUIDE in PageMaker

long as the object is selected, (c) another part of the document is shown (cross-referencing). Figure 3–16 shows these options for the version of GUIDE used in the PageMaker program from Aldus.

Figure 3–17 shows how GUIDE is used as a help system in the PageMaker program. Hypertext allows any text item to act as a "trigger" for various kinds of help information and actions.

Summary

Help systems in commercially available products range from the simple to the sublime. Static help systems (e.g., CROSSTALK and MCI MAIL) probably represent the most typical type of help system in use; they are inexpensive and quick to develop. The most common form of context-sensitive helps are those that are tied to the current function or field selected (such as LOTUS 1–2–3, MELVYN, or VM SCHEDULE). Help systems that use more elaborate techniques such as prompting (SHERPA), embedded documentation (e.g., SYMBOLICS) or hypertext (e.g., GUIDE) are not currently widespread. However, as software users become more demanding and software designers become more sophisticated, it is likely that the help systems provided in commercial products will become increasingly powerful.

4

Research on Helps

Only a few of the many questions about the design and effectiveness of help systems have been the subject of empirical research. There are two fundamental issues: (a) What works and what doesn't? and (b) How can the effectiveness of helps be measured? These two questions are highly interdependent because effectiveness measures are used to determine what works and what doesn't.

Chapter 4 reviews some of the research findings on helps. It also discusses relevant research in the areas of cognitive psychology and artificial intelligence.

Experimental Results

Some of the questions that have been investigated experimentally are:

1. Are different types of helps needed for novices and experts?
2. Which is more effective: user or system-initiated helps?
3. Are online helps more effective than offline helps?
4. What specific features of helps are most helpful?

Relles (1979) conducted one of the first formal studies of help systems. He asked participants to carry out tasks on a simplified bank account management system. The participants were divided into four groups: (a) a control group had a printed manual but no online aids; (b) the second group had the manual and a simple (single-level) help system available; (c) the third group had the manual and a sophisticated (context-sensitive, multilevel) help system available; and (d) the fourth group had the sophisticated help system available but no manual.

Relles ran the experiment twice: first with a group of 6 computer-naive students, and then with a group of 30 computer-experienced students. Relles reported that the computer novices did poorly with the online aids relative to the control group that used the manual only. On the other hand, the groups with computer experience and the sophisticated helps available did better on the tasks than the control group. The availability of the online aids also increased the confidence of the experienced computer groups that they could use the system without the manual.

Cohill and Williges (1985) studied three variables: (a) user versus system initiation of help messages; (b) user versus system selection of help topics, and (c) online versus offline presentation. They studied the performance of 72 novice users of a text editor in a series of text editing tasks. There were eight groups representing all possible combinations of the three variables plus a control group that had no helps available. The results are summarized in Table 4–1.

From this Table, it can be seen that the user-initiated, user-selected groups did better than the groups in which the system initiated or selected the helps. The condition in which the presentation of the help information was via printed manual resulted in

Table 4-1. Summary of Results from Cohill & Williges (1985)

Initiation	Selection	Presentation	Time/Task	Errors/Task	Commands/Task
User	User	Manual	293.1	0.4	8.4
User	User	Online	350.9	1.1	13.5
User	System	Manual	442.2	2.0	17.7
User	System	Online	382.2	1.8	17.6
System	User	Manual	367.9	1.3	13.1
System	User	Online	425.9	2.8	15.1
System	System	Manual	399.1	0.9	13.8
System	System	Online	351.5	1.2	13.7
Control			679.1	5.0	20.2

the best overall performance. All conditions involving the use of helps resulted in much better performance than the control condition involving no help.

Borenstein (1985) developed a context-sensitive help system for UNIX called ACRONYM, as well as alternative text messages for the standard UNIX help facilities ("man" and "key") based upon an introductory UNIX textbook. He compared the standard Unix help, the alternative helps, and ACRONYM, along with advice from a human tutor. In the study, Borenstein asked two groups of computer users (one experienced with UNIX and the other with no UNIX experience) to complete a set of 24 tasks (12 using standard UNIX and 12 using UNIX with either the alternative helps, ACRONYM, or the human tutor available). The mean task completion times (in seconds) under the four conditions are shown in Table 4–2.

Borenstein's results indicate that simply improving the quality of the text messages relative to the standard helps produced better performance and that ACRONYM was not significantly more helpful than the static help messages with improved text. The

Table 4-2. Summary of Results from Borenstein (1985)

Condition	Expert	Novice
Standard UNIX	168	167
Alternative Text	116	115
ACRONYM	139	103
Human Tutor	103	60

help provided by the human tutor was superior to the online helps and much more effective with novice users of UNIX than experienced users.

Magers (1983) tested an improved version of the VAX/VMS operating system with 30 computer novices in a task that involved file manipulation. The improvements included supplementing the help command with a help key, providing context-sensitive helps instead of keyword-indexed helps, making the syntax of help commands more flexible, adding tutorial information to the help messages, eliminating computer jargon in the messages, using examples instead of abstract notation to explain command syntax, providing a dictionary of command synonyms, paging of help messages instead of scrolling, and rewriting the help messages to be task-oriented. The results of the experiment are summarized in Table 4–3.

Mager's results show that the improvements she made had a dramatic effect on performance in the task. The users of the modified system took less time to complete the task, used more commands (approximately twice as many per minute), made fewer errors in the commands they used, used help more often, consulted the manual less often, and asked fewer questions.

What conclusions can be drawn from these experimental studies? It appears that the effectiveness of a help system can vary with the amount of computer experience possessed by the user. However, it is clear from these studies that a well-designed help system can be effective with novice users. It also appears that offline help (i.e., printed manuals) can be more effective than poorly designed online helps but that well-designed helps can produce better performance than offline helps. Finally, it appears

Table 4-3. Summary of Results from Magers (1983)

Measure	Original System	Modified System
Total time (min.)	75.6	52.0
Total commands	70.8	98.5
Commands/min	0.99	1.95
Commands with errors	37.9	17.9
Total Helps	22.4	60.8
References to manuals	11.1	1.8
Questions asked	6.4	2.0

that user control of help messages is better than system control, at least for noncriticial help messages.

With respect to effectiveness measures, total or average task-completion time seems to be the most commonly used performance dimension. Other measures include number of errors made, number of commands used, number of helps required, number of questions asked, and number of references to offline documentation. In general, all of these measures are interdependent, that is, improving the performance on one measure also improves performance on the others. However, it is possible for helps to have specific effects that affect only selected measures.

Experimental studies are useful in formulating design guidelines and providing research paradigms for studying certain questions. However, they are often not of practical value because they examine too few, or too many, variables. In the development of actual systems, the most important kind of experiments are those conducted with prototypes as part of the product development cycle (see Chapter 5). These experiments yield specific answers that can be applied to the design of actual programs and systems.

Discussion of additional studies on helps can be found in Houghton (1984) and Shneiderman (1987).

Cognitive Psychology

Research and theory in cognitive psychology deal with the mental processes involved in perception, attention, memory, problem solving, concept formation, and language. All of these mental processes are obviously relevant to learning and using computer programs and hence the design of help systems. Cognitive psychology also concerns itself with the subject of individual differences—another aspect of obvious relevance to the design of helps.

General principles. There is one aspect of helps that cognitive psychology should be especially valuable for: the issue of when helps are likely to be needed in a program. Elsewhere in the book, we have emphasized that the question of when and where helps are needed is primarily empirical in nature—to be determined by collecting data on people as they use a program and have problems. (Chapter 5 discusses the data collection process in more detail). However, it would be highly desirable to be able to predict when and where helps are needed on the basis of principles of human behavior. Can this be done?

The answer is, not really. Even though there have been many decades of research in cognitive psychology (see Estes, 1975–78; Eysenck, 1975; Aitkenhead & Slack, 1986), there are only a small number of principles that have emerged as generally applicable across all cognitive activities. Here is a sample list:

1. The number of items that a person can attend to or remember for a short time is limited to about seven things ("chunking").
2. People acquire skills better if learning is distributed over time rather than being continuous ("distributed versus massed practice").
3. When recognizing or learning something, people tend to generalize from what they already know ("stimulus generalization").
4. Learning something new that is similar to something already known results in interference between the two items ("negative transfer").
5. When problem solving, people do better if they break the overall problem down into smaller parts and solve those ("subgoal generation").
6. When understanding language, meaning (semantics) generally prevails over the exact form (syntax) of the language.

General principles such as these can be used to make guesses about where helps may be needed in a program. For example, here is a list of conjectures based upon the principles listed above:

1. Any sequence or screen that requires the user to remember or attend to more than five items simultaneously is likely to need a help.
2. Any complex sequence or program that is learned in a single session rather than across multiple sessions is likely to require helps.
3. Any program that works significantly differently from the way a task is done manually or the way other programs work is likely to need helps.
4. If different functions in a program resemble each other but work differently (or similar functions do not resemble each other), helps are likely to be required.

5. Any program that combines a number of steps together instead of allowing the separate steps to be completed individually is likely to require helps.
6. Displays or commands in which the exact format of the information is more important than the content are likely to need helps.

Although such conjectures may be useful in the preliminary design of helps, they are unlikely to provide the kind of detailed guidance needed to develop specific help messages. The major problem in applying general cognitive principles is recognizing the places in a program where a principle might be applied.

More specific models of cognitive processess such as ACT* (Anderson, 1983) or GOMS (Card, Moran, & Newell, 1983) could potentially be more useful than general cognitive psychology principles. For example, Elkerton (1987) has proposed the use of the GOMS model to predict four levels of user assistance: (a) information about goals, (b) information about operations, (c) information about methods, and (d) information about the selection of methods. Because models such as ACT* and GOMS are procedural in nature, they can be used to identify exactly what kind of problem the user might have for a given program sequence.

Errors. There are two research areas in cognitive psychology that have particular relevance to help systems: error theory and mental models. If we had a good theory of how and why people make errors when performing a task, we should be able to use this theory to predict where helps will be needed. Alas, no general theory of errors exists. Bailey (1983) and Norman (1983) have discussed errors people make using computer systems and the implications for design.

Norman distinguishes between mistakes and slips. He points out that slips are a consequence of lack of attention and can occur with beginners or experts alike. Typical slips in using a computer program include pressing the wrong keys or typing the wrong command or file name. Mistakes occur because of misunderstanding or misinterpretation of a situation. Norman proposes that computer systems should try to pinpoint the error and help the user recover as easily as possible.

Helps can assist people in recovering from errors made due to slips by explaining what the problem is. (Systems can also be designed to reduce the chances of slips through the use of "see and point" rather than "remember and type" interfaces). Helps are usually aimed at mistakes that involve misunderstanding or lack of information. Helps should be preemptive in dealing with potential errors, that is, they should require the user to reaffirm their action and warn of possible negative outcomes. For example, when a user types the command: del *.* (delete all files on the disk) in the DOS operating system, the system replies with the message, Are you sure (Y/N)? Similarly, on most systems, when you try to quit or close a file without having saved the file, a message appears asking you if you want to save the file.

A number of researchers have conducted detailed studies of people learning to use computer systems and described the kind of problems encountered. Carroll and colleagues at the IBM T.J. Watson Research Center (Carroll, 1982; Carroll & Carrithers, 1984; Carroll & Mazur,1986) have used protocol analysis techniques in a number of different applications to discover exactly what problems users encounter. For example, in studying new users learning a word processing program, Carroll and Carrithers reported the following seven types of errors:

1. *The exotic menu choice error.* Users tried out all menu options and got lost or hopelessly confused.
2. *The print first error.* Users tried to print documents before they were created and stored.
3. *The parameter loop error.* Users avoided selecting default parameters and got confused selecting parameters they didn't understand.
4. *The alternate shift error.* Users failed to depress both the alternate and shift keys (the cancel operation) and performed undesired operations.
5. *The print queue error.* Users didn't understand the concept of a print queue, causing confusion.
6. *The diskette name error.* Users misnamed the disk being used and were unable to recover from this error.
7. *The unprintable character error.* Users created unprintable characters (which printed out as underscores) in their documents and had difficulty removing them.

Many of these problems are attributable to design flaws in the word processing program which should have been detected and changed before releasing the program. However, others could be found with new users of any program, for example, the exotic menu choice or parameter loop errors. Carroll and Carrithers (1984) suggest a "training wheels" strategy to counteract such errors. The training wheels strategy involves providing new users with an interface in which functions or options are enabled only as needed; other selections are not shown or are inoperable. This approach reduces the number of "wrong turns" a new user can make and hence the chance of errors.

Studying the types of errors people make when using computers (either in general or with specific programs) provides a basis for the design of effective helps. Many help requests made by users (especially novices) are for information to correct errors. A well-designed help system will try to anticipate such errors and provide suitable guidance. A well-designed user interface will minimize errors—reducing the need for error-recovery helps.

Mental models. Research on mental models (Gentner & Stevens, 1983; Johnson-Laird, 1983) is potentially important to the design of help systems because it is believed that people use such models when learning and using programs. If we knew how to analyze the model a user creates when learning a program, we could predict what kinds of problems they would have with the program (i.e., the discrepancies between their model and how the program actually works).

Despite the popularity of the mental model concept and the intuitive logic of the matching hypothesis, there is relatively little data to support it. Kellogg and Breen (1987) used a hierarchical clustering technique to compare the mental models of novices and experts to the actual structure of a text editor. They found that the experts model of the system corresponded relatively closely to the actual system structure, whereas there was less correspondence with the models of the novices.

Lehner and Zirk (1987) compared the performance of two groups of users in an expert systems task. One group was provided with a description of how the expert system worked, whereas the other group was not. The group that was provided with the appropriate mental model performed much better than the group that had to make up their own models.

These two experiments represent three different approaches to the potential use of mental models to improve software usability.

In the first approach, you attempt to map the existing model of the user and determine how it differs from the actual system model. In the second approach, you try to get the user to adopt a model that will minimize problems. A third approach is to allow users to customize the system to match their own model. Current research does not allow us to draw conclusions about the relative merits of these three approaches, or even the viability of the mental model concept.

Individual differences. Although the literature on the subject of individual differences is vast (e.g., Dillon & Schmeck, 1985; Royce & Powell, 1983), relatively little research has been conducted in the context of using computer systems. The number of dimensions that individuals differ on is quite large, including gender, age, education, ethnic/cultural background, aptitudes, learning styles, and personality traits.

Studies suggest that some of these dimensions do have systematic effect on the use of computers. Ambardar (1984) explored the significance of field dependence/field independence (a cognitive style dimension) on performance in a checkbook balancing task. Ambardar found that individuals classified as field dependent preferred a sequential item search mode whereas field-independent individuals preferred a keyword search mode. This preference was measured by the number of times individuals used each mode. In addition, individuals showed faster search times with their preferred search mode, indicating that cognitive styles could affect performance. Ambardar suggested that the difference may be due to the amount of task structure desired by the two types of individuals: field-dependent individuals prefer a more structured problem-solving environment, whereas field-independent individuals prefer a more unstructured environment.

Yoder (1986) investigated the relationship between an individual's cognitive style as measured by the Myers-Brigg Type Indicator and their performance on two tasks using the IBM VM/SP and VM/CMS operating systems. She developed five different formats of help messages that varied along the dimensions of prose versus graphical, explanations versus examples, and directive versus tutorial. Participants in the study were asked to complete the task using the help system as their only source of guidance. Total completion time, number of help requests, and errors made were measured as well as the participant's preferences for the different help formats.

While it was difficult to draw firm conclusions because of the small number of participants (36) and the large number of possible cognitive style categories (16), there were some suggestive results regarding preferences for certain formats depending upon cognitive styles. For example, almost all of the Extraverts preferred graphic formats and most categories of Introverts preferred explanatory formats. Perhaps of more importance, was the finding that most participants performed better with formats based upon examples and poorly using help messages involving abstract explanations.

Differences in ability and skill dimensions can also have effects on performance. Gomez, Egan, and Bowers (1986) studied first-time users of a text editor and looked at the effects of age and spatial ability memory ability on learning rate. Older people and individuals scoring low on a test of spatial memory had more trouble learning to use the text editor. Vicente, Hayes, and Williges (1987) found that spatial visualization ability made a significant difference in a file searching task. Individuals with low spatial ability took twice as long to perform the task as those with high spatial ability. Analysis of command usage indicated that the individuals with low spatial ability were getting lost in the hierarchial file structure.

The difficulty, from the perspective of designing help systems, is how to detect the particular characteristics of the user. Most personality differences are too complex to measure in any simple fashion (lengthy tests are usually used). The best practical strategy is to study carefully the user population and note any systematic and reoccurring differences among users. Then, build the program with the capability for the user to change parameters or functions that are important to them.

For example, suppose it was known that a significant portion of users were older individuals with various types of visual impairments. A "large display" or "zoom" option could be provided that presents all screens in a magnified size, hence increasing the readability of the displays. Or, imagine an electronic conferencing system used by both introverts and extraverts. Suppose that extremely introverted people like to compose their replies and comments in private before posting them, whereas very extroverted people like to compose messages in public view. A system could be designed to accomodate both personality types by allowing both private and public composition.

Providing multiple options and user customization is a good way of dealing with individual differences, as well as providing a flexible interface for all users. However, in order to know what individual differences are important for a given system or application, detailed analysis of the user population is needed.

As a final comment on individual differences, it is worth noting the conclusions of Card, Moran and Newell (1983) in their study of the cognitive psychology of text editing. Although they did find significant individual differences across individuals according to level of experience, they concluded that the differences were not nearly as great as the differences across different text editing programs within the same experience levels. In other words, performance differences due to the design of the software overshadowed differences due to experience. Perhaps this supports the hypothesis that a good help system may compensate for individual differences by allowing users to explore a system in whatever fashion is most suitable to them.

Artificial Intelligence

A good case can be made for the position that one of the reasons why most existing help systems have failed to be very helpful to users is because they are "stupid," that is, they do not understand what the user is trying to do, what the user wants to know, or the meaning of the advice provided. Making help systems "smart" involves the use of artificial intelligence techniques and methodology.

From an artificial intelligence perspective, the central problem in designing a good help system is mapping what the user wants to do onto what the system can do (Mark, 1982). In other words, the system must be able to interpret the intention of the user in performing a certain action so that a meaningful explanation of why it worked/didn't work can be provided. The system must be able to model the user in some fashion in order to understand intention and goals.

An intelligent help system should be able to provide a high level of context sensitivity because it has an understanding of what the user is trying to accomplish. Finin (1983) showed how a help system could recognize when the user needs help on the basis of inefficient or ineffective actions. Rissland, Valcarce and

Ashley (1984) discuss how an intelligent help system should be able to generate examples relevant to the current context.

Fischer, Lemke and Schwab (1985) describe two knowledge-based help systems called PASSIVIST and ACTIVIST, developed to provide assistance while using a text editor. PASSIVIST responds to queries posed by the user in natural language and uses a help strategy in which each step of the solution is presented and explained to the user. For example, the query, "How can I delete the next line?" would generate a set of step-by-step instructions for the user to follow, with each step monitored by the system.

ACTIVIST is a system-initiated help program that tries to understand each user action and identify incorrect actions. Each action performed by the user is matched against plans that specify the correct sequence of events and alternatives for editor functions. Help messages are displayed when an incorrect action is performed for a plan recognized by the system.

The development of any type of intelligent help system requires the implementation of rules to determine what advice to give the user. Aaronson and Carroll (1987) studied the nature of the brief messages exchanged between users and human advisors of an electronic mail system. They identified a number of strategies used by the advisors to decide how to help the user. These strategies included (a) make assumptions about the goals of the user and base the answer on the assumption made, (b) provide alternative solutions when the goal is not clear, (c) assume a configuration when this is unspecified, (d) advise the user to do something else to avoid the problem, and (e) provide reference sources when the problem seemed too complex to explain in a short reply. Furthermore, Aaronson and Carroll identified additional strategies used by the advisors to limit the need for follow-up help messages.

Another major requirement of an intelligent help system is a comprehensive knowledge base of the application or program the help is designed for. If the help system cannot make inferences about how the program works or cannot associate one concept with another, it will not be able to understand help requests. Rich and Morgan (1982) suggests that the actual program itself should be intelligent and be able to deal with questions about its operation. For example, it should be able to explain the cause of an error or outcome by displaying the sequence of operations that led to the error/outcome. An intelligent program should be capable of making comparisons between different alternatives and hence be able to answer "what if" type queries. In essence, the program would have a "subconscious" that allows it to inspect its own operation.

Many researchers feel that natural language understanding is a critical aspect of building intelligent help systems. Figure 4–1

```
User: How do I delete a file?
UC: Typing 'rm filename' will remove
      the file with name filename from
      your current directory.
User: What is the best way to create
      a file?
UC: The best way to create a new file
      is to use the editor, i.e., 'ex filename'.
User: a directory?
UC:   Typing 'mkdir directoryname' will
      create a directory with the name
      directoryname in your current
      directory.
User: How can I make changes to a file?
UC:   Typing 'ex filename' will get you
      into the ex editor; typing 'emacs
      filename' will get you into the
      emacs editor.
User: How can I find out how full the disk
      is?
UC:   Typing 'df' will tell you how full the
      disk is.
```

Figure 4–1. Dialog with Unix Consultant

shows the type of help dialog possible with a natural language system. The system is called UC (the UNIX Consultant) and it is designed to provide assistance with UNIX operating system.

Wilensky, Arens, and Chin (1984) describe the major components required to build a system like UC: a language analyzer and generator, a context and memory mechanism, a knowledge network of facts about UNIX, planning and goal-analysis mechanisms that can reason about the user's intentions, and a UC Teacher that would allow UC to learn more about UNIX via natural language.

Artificial intelligence research holds much promise for the design of more effective help systems. However, at present, the amount of time and special expertise required to build such systems keeps them in the research domain and out of the practical realm. This is likely to change as artificial intelligence techniques become part of mainstream computing.

Summary

This chapter has surveyed some of the lines of research that are relevant to help systems. Experimental studies of helps have investigated factors such as relative effectiveness with novice and experts, user versus system-initiated messages, static versus dynamic helps, and online versus offline messages. The research suggests that the quality of help messages is one of the most important variables in determining effectiveness.

Research in cognitive psychology has identified a number of basic principles of human behavior that can be used to predict what type of helps may generally be required. Studies of human error also indicate the kinds of helps that may be needed in a system. The study of mental models created by users about systems may also be useful in determining the kinds of problems users may encounter.

Research on individual differences indicates that some dimensions of ability and personality appear to affect how well people use computers. It is suggested that individual differences should be accommodated by allowing users to customize interface parameters—including help systems.

Artificial intelligence research has focused on the development of help systems that understand what the user is doing and what kind of help is needed. The ability to phrase help requests in natural language is an important aspect of this research.

The research discussed in this chapter can provide useful ideas for the design of a help system. However, these ideas must be implemented and tested in a specific program as part of the product development cycle. Chapter 5 outlines this process.

5

Implementation

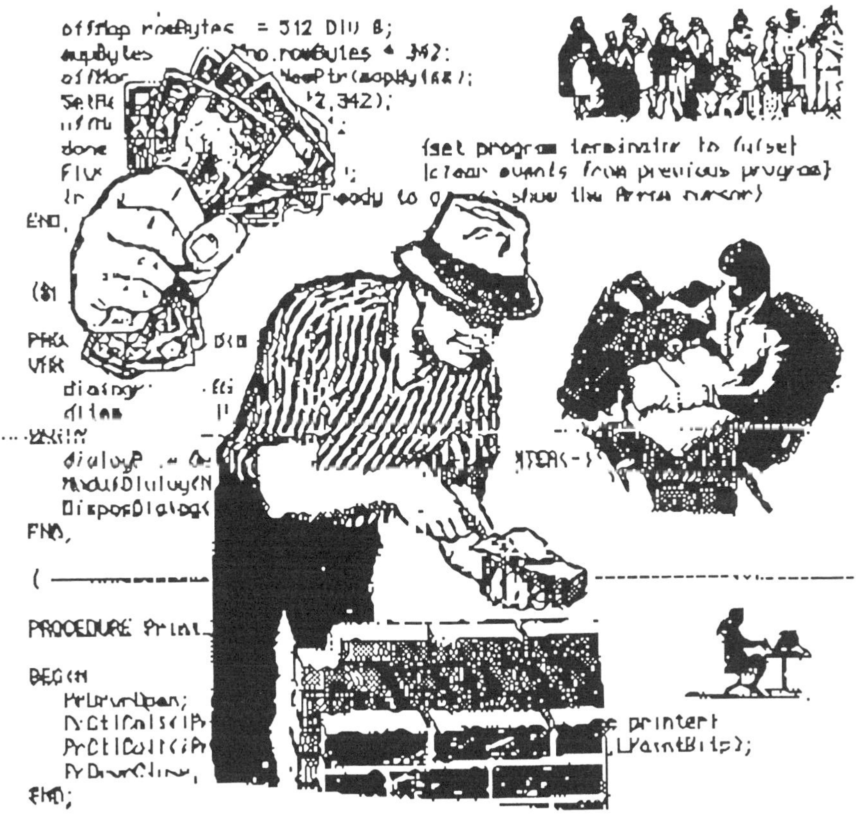

In Chapter 5 we discuss the implementation aspects of help systems including requirements analysis, prototyping, coding/writing, user tryouts, quality control, maintenance, and cost/benefits analysis.

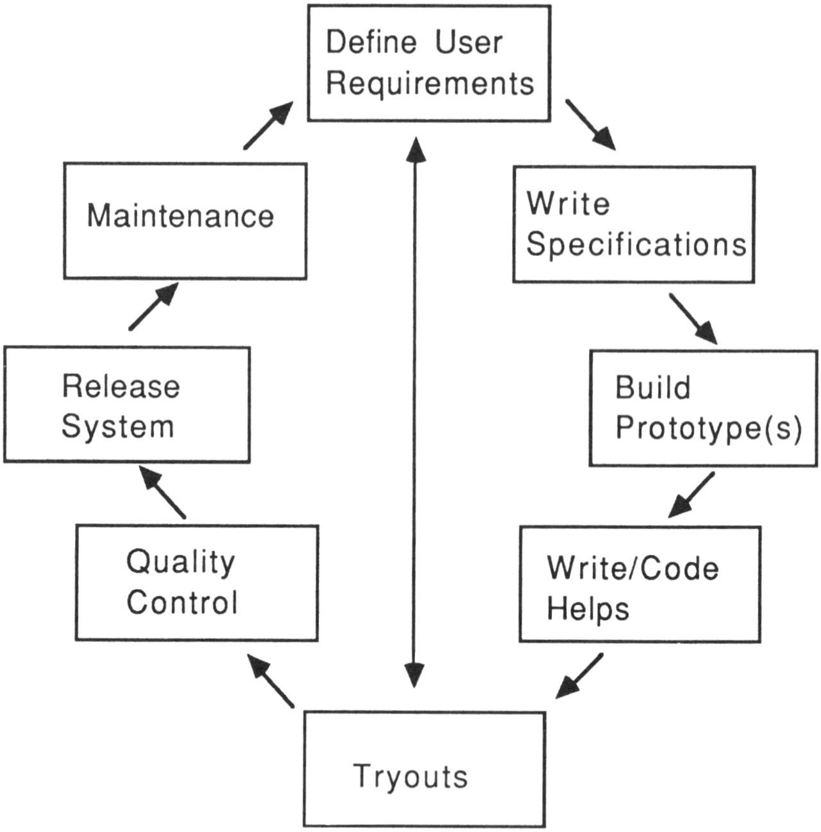

Figure 5–1. Help System Implementation Cycle

Figure 5–1 outlines the major steps in the implementation cycle for help systems. Anyone with software development experience will recognize that the steps are the same as those involved in implementing any program or system. Which is exactly the point: implementing a help system requires the same amount of effort and all the steps that the full fledged system entails.

Two important things to keep in mind about the steps shown in Figure 5–1 are that each step may not always be explicit and steps may happen in a different sequence. For example, the requirements analysis step may be included as part of the specification definition step. Prototyping may be conducted as part of the specification or tryout steps. Figure 5–1 shows an idealized sequence that will differ in practice from project to project.

Analyzing User Requirements

The beginning step in the cycle should be the analysis of user requirements. Like any other component of well-designed software, helps must respond to specific user needs. To identify these needs, it is usually necessary to collect data using techniques such as task analysis, critical incidents, protocol analysis, focus groups, surveys, or, simply, observation. Figure 5–2 describes these techniques. On the other hand, if the program already exists in some form, the data needed may already be available from trouble reports collected via hotlines or feedback forms.

The main concern in analyzing user requirements is to identify

Task Analysis
Identifying all tasks required to successfully complete a job or activity and the order in which they must be completed.

Critical Incidents
Successful and unsuccessful incidents associated with a specified activity are listed and then sorted to reveal commonalities.

Focus Groups
Small groups of prospective users are given a description or shown a prototype of a product idea and asked for their reactions.

Protocol Analysis
Individual users are asked to describe aloud what they are doing and thinking when using a program and these descriptions are transcribed.

Time & Motion
All input actions (i.e., keypresses) are logged along with the duration of each action and wait times.

Figure 5–2. Techniques Used to Collect User Requirements Data

where and why users have (or are likely to have) problems in a program. Some things can be taken for granted, such as the need for explanations of the correct syntax and use of commands. However, even in this case, it is not obvious how much information users want or how the helps should be accessed.

One common outcome of conducting a requirements analysis for a help system is that shortcomings in the program are revealed. Some problems may be better handled by program modifications rather than by helps. Any problem which is consistently experienced by the majority of users points to a program deficiency as opposed to a help.

Zemke and Kramlinger (1983) provide a good introduction to the different techniques that can be used to identify user requirements.

Specifications

The information collected from the user requirements analysis should be used to write a set of help specifications. These specifications should define the overall design of the help system in terms of the alternatives discussed in Chapter 2 (i.e., static vs. dynamic, levels, access method, user vs. system initiation, screen formating, etc.). In the case of dynamic helps, the algorithm(s) for identifying the appropriate help message must be specified.

In addition to these general design considerations, the following details must also be specified:

- *The size and location of the help message.* The help window should be large enough to display the longest help message (or be designed to have multiple pages). It can be located in a fixed area on the screen or be a pop-up window that is positioned anywhere.
- *The response made by the user to activate/remove the help.* The user should be able to press a single key (or click the mouse) to get help and then continue with the application.
- *How the help messages are to be stored.* The best technique is to store helps as text files external to the program. This allows them to be created and modified without affecting the program.

- *The methodology to be used to quality control helps.* How helps will be validated and who will do this.
- *The procedure for updating helps.* How often and who has responsibility for keeping helps up to date.

The specification should also provide an estimate of the amount of time required to program and test the help system and the time required to write and edit the help messages.

Prototyping

A prototype is a mock-up or model of something. Prototypes do not have to work like the actual product, nor do they need to be complete. Prototyping has become a important activity in software interface design as a means of examining alternative designs There are many screen generation, authoring systems, and slideshow programs available that make prototype development relatively fast and easy (see Appendix B).

In the design of help systems, prototyping can be used to explore the effectiveness of alternative help designs before development begins. Actual screens from the application program can be captured or recreated and simulated help options/messages added to these screens. In a prototype it is not necessary to include all application screens or have a full set of help messages. Different prototypes can be created using the same application screens with different types of helps. Because prototypes can be developed quickly and at a small cost, they encourage the comparison of design alternatives.

Prototypes of help systems can be used in tryouts to collect preliminary data on the effectiveness of helps, or can be used in requirements analysis to get user reactions to helps. They can also be used to examine the feasibility or obtain development estimates for ideas in a specification.

Coding/writing

Assuming that the specifications have been finalized, the next step is to actually develop the help system. This involves two different tasks: coding the help system and writing the help messages. The first task is a programming job; the second is communication. In most cases, different people will be needed for each task.

There are two different ways that help systems can be programmed. The most common is for the help routines to be coded in the same programming language used for the application program. This makes it easier to integrate the help routines with the program and also simplifies maintenance. However, for this approach to work, it is usually necessary that the help capabilities be included in the program design from the outset. Trying to add help capabilites after the system has been completed is usually difficult and time consuming.

An alternative approach is to use an authoring or window creation tool that produces memory resident routines that can be run concurrently with the application program. There are many such authoring tools available for personal computers (see Appendix B). The advantage of this approach is that the help system can be developed independent of the application. Thus, it is possible for the help system to be developed in parallel with the application program and then added once the program is in final form. The main disadvantage of this approach is that the particular form and features of the help system are determined by the authoring tool. There also may be licensing considerations associated with authoring tools.

Help messages need to be written by a communication specialist (e.g., technical writer, instructional designer). A great deal of effort is usually required to get exactly the right wording for help messages. Help messages should be concise but easy to understand—the type of writing style exhibited by good journalists. The language used should be simple and free of jargon/terminology. Readability of help messages can be improved by using short paragraphs, ragged right margins, tabular layouts, and ample white space.

Tryouts

Tryouts involve testing preliminary or prototype help systems with small groups of prospective users. Data from such tryouts can be collected in a number of different ways. The analysis techniques mentioned in the section on requirements analysis and listed in Figure 5–2 apply to the tryout step as well. Response data can also be collected by the system so that the number and nature of errors, time to complete transactions, and response latency is known for each user. This provides very comprehensive and detailed information on whether a help system is effective or not.

Another important kind of data that should be collected during tryouts is user attitudes. Attitude data can be collected by online or printed questionnaires. Some typical questions are:

- Did you find the program easy or difficult to use?
- What problems did you have using the program?
- Did you find the helps useful? Why/Why not?
- How could the helps be improved?

Questions can be asked in open response format as shown above or with response scales (Agree/Disagree) if quantitative data is desired.

Data collected from tryouts should be used to determine the final form of a help system or the format of help messages. It should identify help messages that are missing or existing messages that need rewriting.

Quality Control

Quality control involves a careful review or inspection of the help system to detect any potential problems and correct any mistakes. Quality review of help systems should cover two major activities: bullet proofing of help requests and proofing of the help messages.

Bullet proofing means an exhaustive testing of all help options to ensure that help requests always work. This involves testing a variety of accidental or unlikely situations, such as selecting helps with the num or caps lock key on, while printing, if the mouse fails, or the wrong function/control keys are pressed. Another important aspect of bullet proofing activity is to test the help system with different hardware and operating system configurations. Many programs are used with a variety of terminals or personal computers, and it is necessary to check out each variation.

Unfortunately, there is no systematic way to do bullet proofing. A checklist can be created on the basis of past experience and each item on the checklist tested. However, good bullet proofing depends upon a more or less random exploration of unlikely occurrences. For this reason, people who are not familiar with the program (or computers in general), often produce the best results for bullet proofing.

Proofing involves checking the text of all help messages for correct spelling and grammar as well as clear writing and good style. The standard rules of good writing should be followed:

- Use short sentences.
- Use the active voice.
- Provide lots of examples.
- Use tables when possible.

Accuracy of helps is very important because users will rely on the information provided by helps. For this reason, it is critical that the text of help messages be as correct as possible. When an incorrect help is encountered, the credibility of the entire help system is undermined.

Releases

One of the difficulties with software development is that programs are never really finished—there are always more features or options that could be added. For this reason, the concept of a *release* is very important. A release is an agreed-upon set of program features that will completed on a given date. Features that cannot be completed satisfactorily by that date are saved for a subsequent release.

Another important aspect of the release concept is that each set of changes is examined together for interdependencies. It is common for a change to one part of a program to have side effects on other aspects of a program. If each change was distributed individually, interactions among changes are not as likely to be detected.

Help systems, like all other software components, should be developed and distributed as releases. This may mean that only one of multiple levels may be available in an early release or that only static, rather than dynamic helps are initially released.

The release dates and set of features associated with each date need to be made explicit early in a software project so that development schedules can be planned and coordinated.

Maintenance

A major problem with many help systems (as well as documentation and training materials) is that they become out of date and no longer provide accurate information. It is common for a program to undergo many changes in early releases. If the help messages are not revised along with the program, the help messages may give advice or explanations that no longer match the way the program works. Such obsolete help messages cause user confusion and loss of faith in the helps.

To avoid this potential problem, it is essential that all changes in the program be reflected in the helps and that each new release of the program be accompanied by a new release of the help system. The individual(s) responsible for the help system must be kept informed of changes to the program and be given sufficient time to make changes to the helps. This means that those responsible for help systems must participate in product review and planning meetings and be on the distribution list for all product status memoranda/ reports.

From a management perspective, it is important that the implementation of help systems be viewed as an ongoing activity. This means that the budget for development of helps should include adequate funds for maintenance activities. As a rule of thumb, at least 10% of the initial development costs should be allocated each year for maintenance costs over the life cycle of the product.

Cost/benefit Tradeoffs

Prior to and during the help-system implementation cycle, a number of cost/benefit tradeoffs must be made. Help systems take time and resources to implement; this must be weighed against the payoffs of increased usability.

As explained in Chapter 1, the major payoffs of help systems are reduced errors and reduced transaction times. In addition, good helps should reduce the time required to learn a system. Figure 5–3 illustrates how such payoffs can be measured.

The figure shows two versions of a system being compared in terms of average number of errors made and/or average time to

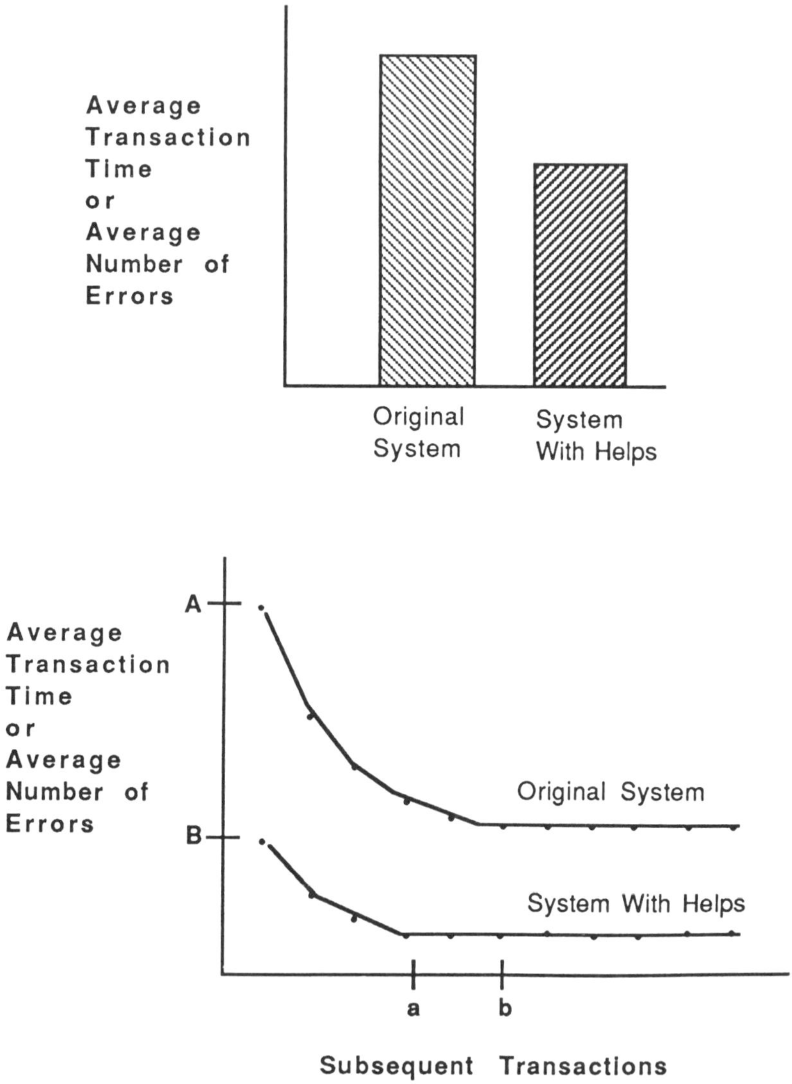

Figure 5–3. Measuring the Effectiveness of Helps for a Specific Program Module (top) or Across Time (bottom)

complete a transaction. In the version of the system with helps, fewer errors are made and it takes less time to complete a task. The bottom part of Figure 5–3 illustrates this result over time (i.e., successive sessions) and represents the learning curve for the system. Note that with helps, the user makes fewer errors and takes less time initially (A vs. B) as well as reaching a "steady state" sooner (a vs. b). Also note that a user can always work faster and make less errors in the version of the system with the helps. In other words, the help system continues to produce better performance even for experienced users.

Although a comparison is usually made between two versions of a system—with and without helps—it could also compare two or more different types of helps to assess the difference in effectiveness between them. In many instances, it will not be possible to decide between alternative help designs on the basis of past research or design principles; a study that compares error rate and completion time will be necessary.

Improvements in the usability are translated into financial benefits in the form of reduced product support and marketing costs. Support costs include the development and distribution of documentation, giving training seminars, and providing customer hotlines. The more usable a program or system is, the less support it will require. Marketing costs include product demonstrations, advertising materials, and packaging. Programs and systems that are easy to use are generally also easier to sell—hence reduced selling time and costs. Although high usability will not eliminate the need for product and marketing support, it can minimize these costs.

The costs involved in implementing helps are the labor costs associated with each step in the implementation cycle. The time required to implement a help system can range from a few weeks to several person years, depending upon the complexity of the help system. The low end would be represented by a single-level, static help system for an existing program in which user problems are well documented. In this case, the help mechanism is very simple, and the data needed to define user needs is easily available. The high end would be represented by a multilevel, dynamic help system for a new type of program. Here, the user requirements will need to be analyzed, and the programming is likely to be fairly involved. In addition, the actual writing of the helps, the tryout process, and maintenance of the help system will probably be lengthy.

Making design decisions about help systems involves balancing the anticipated effectiveness of the helps (in terms of increased program usability) against the labor costs of implementing the design. It is possible to err in two directions—too minimal a design, or too elaborate a design. A design that is too minimal fails to make a significant contribution to the usability of the program. A design that is too elaborate may improve the usability of the program at too great a development cost. The only way to determine the right level is to build prototypes, run tryouts, and collect effectiveness data.

Summary

The implementation cycle for helps includes eight major steps:

1. User requirements analysis
2. Specification definition
3. Prototyping
4. Coding/writing
5. User tryouts
6. Quality control
7. Release
8. Maintenance

Although it is possible to develop help systems without going through all of these steps, the more steps that are completed, the greater the chances of success. Each step makes an important contribution to the implementation of an effective help system.

One aspect of the implementation process for helps that is not always obvious to software designers is the extent to which it depends upon data-collection activities. Two of the most critical steps, namely requirements analysis and tryouts, involve extensive data collection. In addition, prototyping and quality control are likely to be closely associated with data-collection activities in tryouts or initial program tests. Such data-collection activities do not necessarily require formal studies but may consist of careful and continued observation of users throughout the implementation process.

The moral is this: Designers of help systems should be prepared to spend a significant amount of time observing and collecting data on users if they want to do their job well!

6

Guidelines

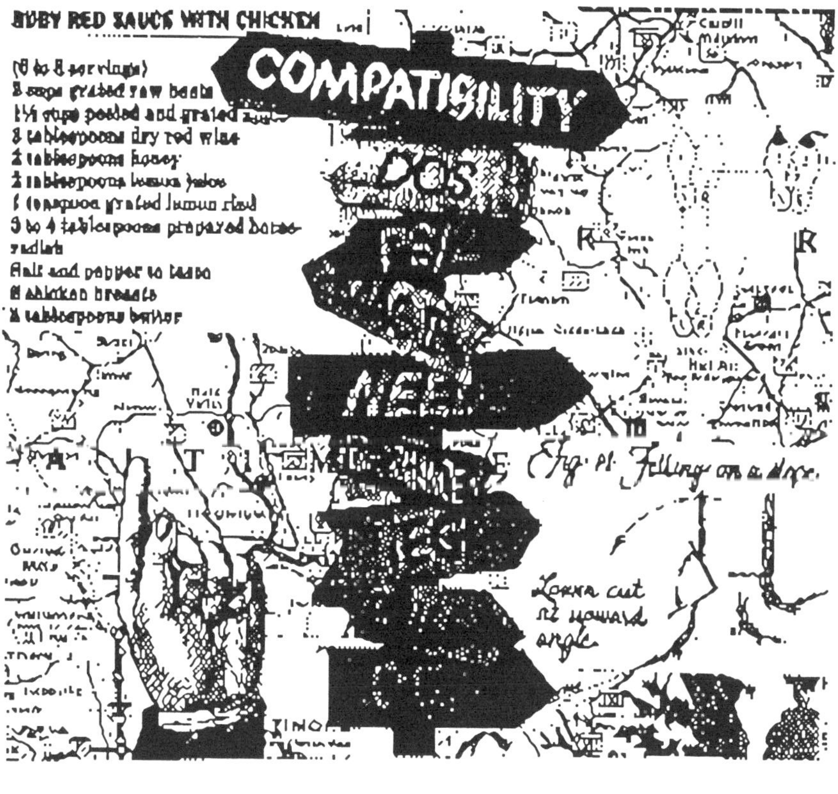

Chapter 6 provides a set of practical guidelines for the design and implementation of help systems. It represents a synthesis of the ideas presented in earlier chapters.

To put this chapter in perspective, it might help to summarize the major problems that users report with existing help systems:

- Difficulty switching between help and application.
- Helps don't provide the specific information desired.
- Help information is not available when needed.
- Help information is not accurate or incomplete.
- Help information is difficult to understand.
- Help system is confusing to use.

The following guidelines address these problems. Throughout this chapter, we use screens from a hypothetical database inquiry system (HRIS) to illustrate the guidelines.

Make the Help System Easy to Access and Easy to Return From

Helps must not add additional problems or make the situation more confusing. A help system that is difficult to use or makes it difficult to return to the application program, will not be considered useful. The user should be able to get help and return to the application with a single keypress or mouse click.

The user should be reminded that help is available by displaying the command or function key to be used to get help. If help is not available at all places or times in the program, a message should indicate when help is/is not available.

Help messages should be displayed in windows overlapping the application or in message areas at the bottom of the screen. A separate help screen that completely replaces the application screen is undesirable because it prevents the user from looking at the problem and help screen simultaneously. On the other hand, overlapping windows that can be resized and repositioned or fixed message areas allow the user to see the help information and the problem at the same time.

Make Helps as Specific as Possible

When people ask for help, they normally have a specific question or problem in mind. They want an answer or explanation that is specific to *that* question or problem. Help systems that involve wading through a lot of irrelevant information are not going to be perceived as very helpful.

In short, the more specific the help, the better. Use the following strategies to make helps specific:

- Allow the help request to be specific, that is, allow users to specify the command/function and options they want explained (e.g., >help print/queue limit or "What is the maximum size of the print/queue").
- Make the help context sensitive, that is, dependent upon what action the user has selected or where the user is in the program.
- Develop multilevel helps and make it easy for the user to specify the level of help they want (e.g., >help/why or >help/example).
- Provide an index and cross-reference helps so the user can explore other topics easily if the initial one selected/presented is not useful.

Figure 6–1 illustrates a context-sensitive help that provides multiple levels of explanation, an index, and easy access/return to the application via function and control keys.

Even a high degree of context sensitivity may not always pro-

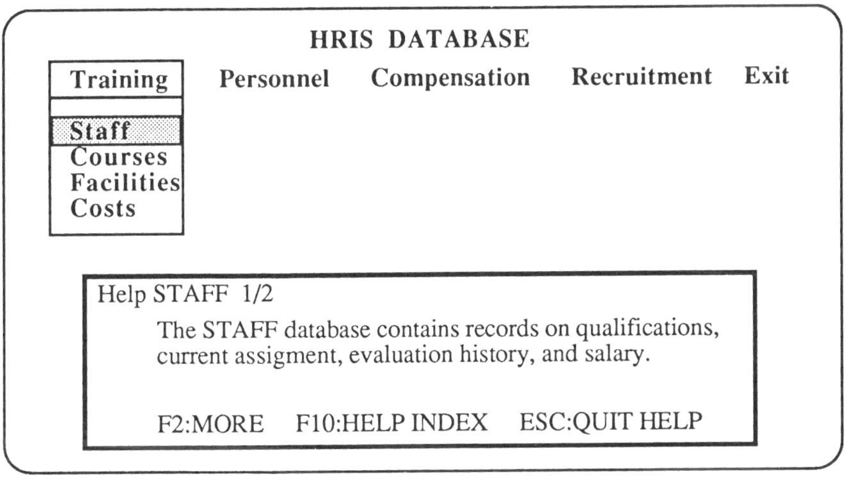

Figure 6–1. Example of Context -Sensitive Help

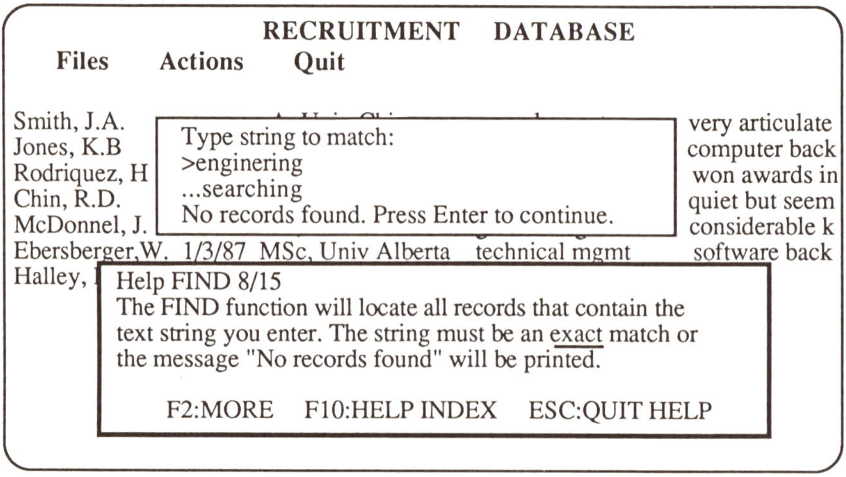

Figure 6–2. Example of Correct But Inadequate Help

vide specific enough help. For example, in Figure 6–2, the user has misspelled the text string ("enginering") and consequently the system has failed to find the record(s). The help message is not very useful since it is not smart enough to recognize the exact problem, although it does state the nature of the problem correctly.

Collect Data to Determine What Helps Are Needed

It can't be emphasized enough that the design of good help systems (and good user interfaces, in general) is critically dependent upon careful analysis of actual user problems. Instead of trying to second guess what kinds of help will needed, develop a prototype and observe what people do. Try these data collection ideas:

- Sit beside (or videotape) users as they try out the prototype and ask them to verbalize anything they don't understand or have problems with. Make copious notes and prompt them to describe what they are doing.
- Insert a data-logging routine in the program that collects user response data including keypresses, time to respond, error messages received, help requests, commands used, and so on.
- Put a comment routine in the program that allows users to log

comments whenever they have a problem. Make sure that the comment capability is easy to use and encourage people to make lots of comments.
- Insert a brief questionnaire in critical parts of the program that asks users to describe any problems they are having with the program, what aspects they find hard to use, and so on.

When analyzing user data, focus your attention on the places where users make errors and the kinds of errors they make. This is likely to give you the best leads about what kinds of helps are needed (and not just helps for error recovery).

Give Users as Much Control of the Help System as Possible

The more control users have over the help system, the more useful they will find it. Users should be able to:

- initiate a help request and select the help topic desired;
- select the level of help, if multiple levels are available; and
- add to or change existing help messages.

Figure 6–3 shows the index for a static help system (i.e., online glossary). The help system has an "ADD" function that lets users

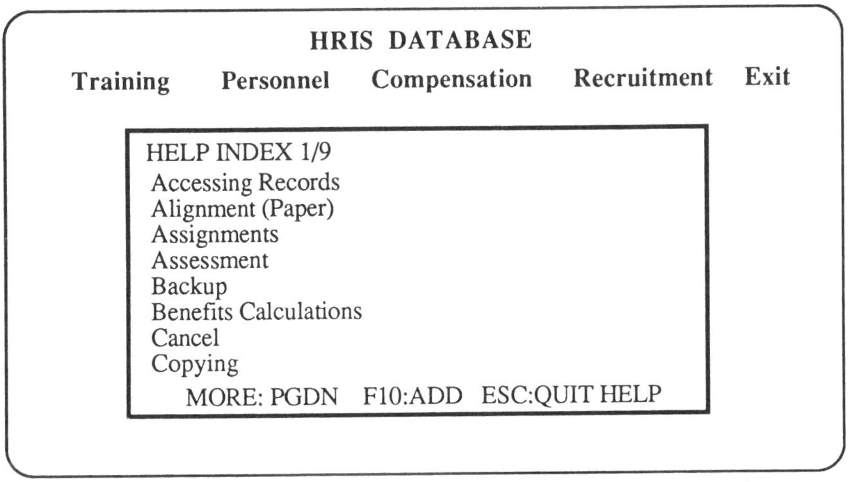

Figure 6–3. Index and Add Function Provide User Control

add their own terms to the help system or add information to existing terms. Both the index and the add function provide user control of the help system.

If the system generates help messages without user initiation, users should have the option of turning off the help system if they don't want to be interrupted by the messages.

Different Types of Users Need Different Helps

Apart from individual differences, users will differ in their degree of computer experience. Here are three types of user groups who probably require different types of helps:

- *Novices.* Users who have little experience with computers will need help with basic concepts and operations. As a rule, novices want to see only information that is absolutely necessary.
- *Experts.* Experienced computer users want to know about limitations, shortcuts, and complex operations. They want to know anything that will allow them to do things more efficiently.
- *Casual users.* People who only use a computer (or the current application) occasionally. They may be either novices or experts. Casual users need help remembering things they already know.

One important thing to keep in mind is that people can switch categories fairly quickly. A person may change from being a novice to an expert on a particular program in a few hours. Someone who was once an expert may become a casual user. Experts on one system may be novices on another. Help systems can accommodate these changes if they allow users to select the level and type of helps (see Figure 6–4).

Help Messages Must be Accurate and Complete

If the user discovers a help message that is inaccurate or misleading, the credibility of the entire help system is suspect (even if all other help messages are fine). It is absolutely essential that all help messages be reviewed for technical accuracy and correct-

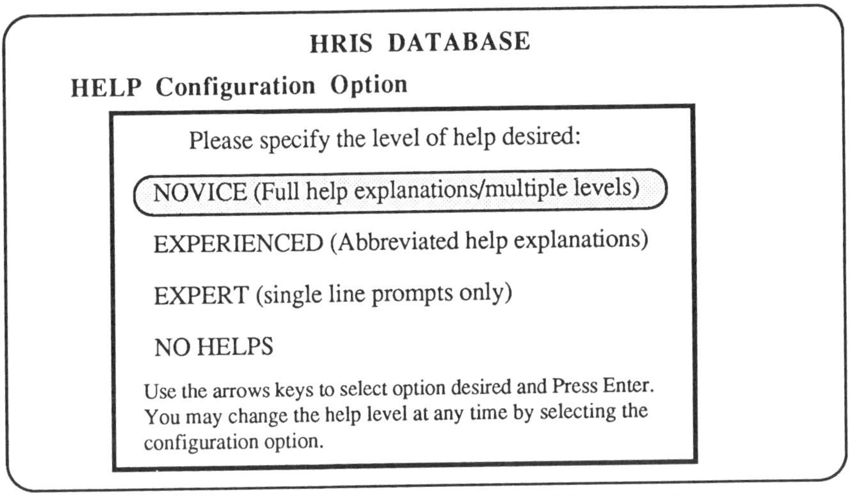

Figure 6–4. Allowing the User to Specify Level of Help

ness. Help messages should also be proof-read by an editor for spelling and grammar mistakes.

A common reason why help messages are inaccurate or incomplete is that they are not updated when changes are made to the program. For this reason, help messages must be reviewed each time a new release of a program is made. Checking that help

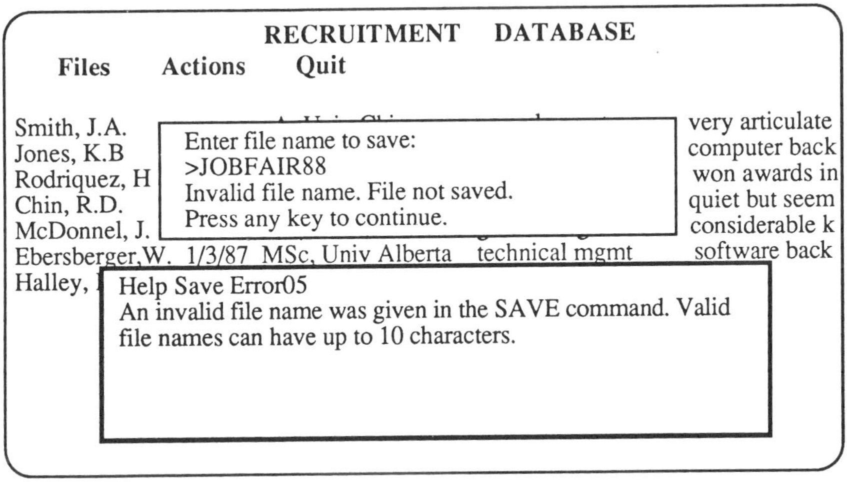

Figure 6–5. An Incomplete and Misleading Help Message

messages have been updated should be a routine step in the quality-control process.

Figure 6–5 illustrates how a help message can be misleading because of incompleteness. The message fails to mention that file names cannot contain numbers (there is nothing wrong with the length of the filename).

Don't Use Helps to Compensate for Poor Interface Design

Help systems are often used as band aids to patch up poorly designed interfaces. Instead of adding more help messages, try rewriting directions, redesigning menus or commands, improving the screen layouts, and better error handling. This may reduce the dependence of the user on the help system.

Although help systems can make a good program better, they will not magically turn a poorly designed program into a good one.

Figure 6–6 illustrates a help system compensating for poor design in the original system. If the system displayed the file names as part of the LOAD function, a problem with a incorrect filename could not occur—and the help wouldn't be needed.

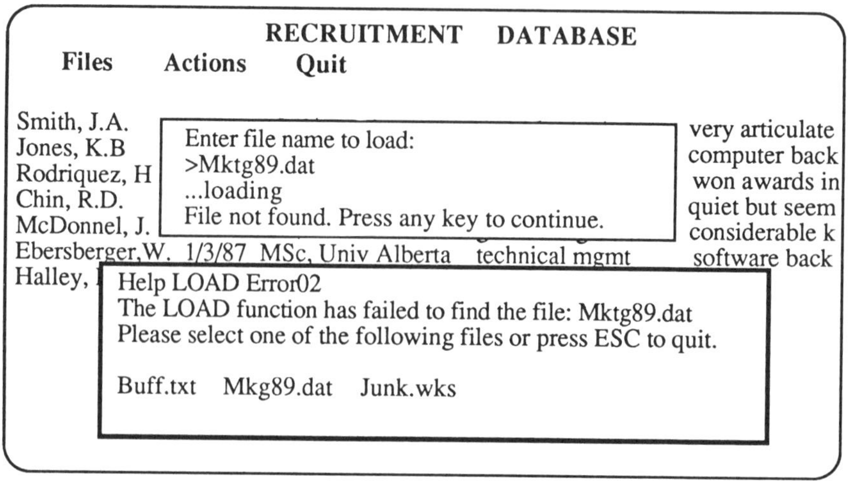

Figure 6–6. Help System Compensates for Poor Inteface Design

Summary

Here are the guidelines suggested in this chapter:

- Make the help system easy to access and easy to return from.
- Make helps as specific as possible.
- Collect data to determine what helps are needed.
- Give the user as much control of the help system as possible.
- Different types of users need different helps.
- Help messages must be accurate and complete.
- Don't use helps to compensate for poor interface design.

Following these guidelines should result in an effective help system and more usable software.

7

Summary & Conclusions

Chapter 7 synthesizes the ideas presented in the preceding chapters. The summary is organized according to the following categories of individuals likely to be involved in the design and implementation of help systems: DP/MIS managers, software designers and developers, training and documentation specialists, researchers, and the rest of us.

Table 7-1. Schedule for Development of Help System

Task	Wk 1	Wk 2	Wk 3	Wk 4	Wk 5 . . . end
1. Identify user requirements	xx				
2. Write help specifications	xx				
3. Build/evaluate prototypes		xxxx			
4. Write and code helps		xxxxxxx			
5. Tryout help system			xxx		
6. Quality control helps				xx	
7. Release initial system				x	
8. Revise/update helps				xxxxxxxx	

For DP/MIS Managers

For the manager of data processing or management information systems in an organization, help systems have the following significance: They increase the usability of application programs and reduce the amount of training/user support required.

The design of a help system can be a lengthy and complex process. Feedback from user tryouts with prototypes should be used to determine which features are most important for a given application. The mistakes made and the problems identified in such tryouts indicate where helps are needed and what kind.

A common reason why helps systems are inadequately developed (or not developed at all), is the failure of project/product managers to schedule and budget for all the necessary implementation steps. Table 7–1 provides a hypothetical example of a development schedulinge for a help system.

Note that in a real schedule, the tasks would usually be broken down into more detailed subtasks. The actual duration of each task will depend upon the size of the system and the experience of the developer(s).

One important thing to notice in Table 7–1 is that maintenance responsibilities extend over the entire lifetime of the program. Each time a revision is made to the application, the helps will likely need to be updated and revised. It is very important to plan for, and assign, this responsibility when implementing a help system.

As a general rule, the greater the consequences of user mistakes or poor performance, the more important the help system becomes. For example, help systems are highly critical in real-time systems such as those used for online banking and travel reservations, emergency and life-support systems, process control, or weapons systems. In such systems, the user cannot afford to take time to look things up in offline documentation or call someone else for assistance.

Furthermore, the greater the variance in the backgrounds or experience of users, the more important the help system becomes, because the chance of misunderstanding or misinterpretation increases. It is much easier to design a system for users who have common backgrounds and expectations than for a diverse group.

Another thing to keep in mind when implementing a help system is that a variety of different kinds of skills are involved, hence you are likely to need different individuals for different tasks. For example, identifying user requirements involves good analysis and interview skills. Writing and quality controlling the help messages requires someone with good language and editing ability (as well as a thorough understanding of the application). To design the actual help system, a software designer with user interface design experience is needed. Because it is highly unlikely that you will find a single person who combines all of the different skills required, a team approach is usually necessary.

For Software Designers/Developers

The major challenge for a software designer or developer when creating a help system is to make good decisions about designthe many alternatives possible. Table 7–2 summarizes the various choices to be made based on the discussion in Chapter 2.

The research and examples discussed in Chapters 2 and 3, as well as the guidelines presented in Chapter 6, should give you some idea of which design alternatives apply to a specific project. However, only analysis of user requirements and error data collected from tryouts will tell you exactly where helps are needed and what kind.

In many cases, you will not be able to decide between two equally plausible design alternatives. This is one of the major reasons for using prototypes. Create identical program sequences or segments that differ only in the design alternatives under consideration and run some tryouts. Collect data on task duration,

Table 7-2. Design Alternatives for Help Systems

- Static versus dynamic
  - fixed messages
  - last response/action
  - specific to current function
  - sequence of user actions
- Multiple levels
  - more detailed explanations
  - structural organization
  - specific parameters/options
- Control structures
  - typed commands
  - help keys
  - menu options
  - hypertext
- System versus user initiation
  - triggered by error conditions or irreversible actions
  - user control of system-initiated helps
- Screen formatting
  - location/size of message area
  - paging versus scrolling
  - use of windowing
- Extensibility
  - user editing capabilities
  - user customization of help options
- Other considerations
  - file structures
  - printing capabilities
  - bookmarking capability
  - networking access
  - hardware/software contraints

errors made, learning time, user preferences, and so on. If there are significant differences between the design alternatives, they should show up in your data. If you cannot detect any differences, then you can conclude that, from a usability perspective, it doesn't matter which alternative is selected. Of course, there may be other factors to use in making a decision such as implementation difficulty or space/speed considerations.

A final design consideration to keep in mind is maintainability. Help systems that are not continually updated and revised as the application program changes quickly become useless. In most cases, it is the content of the help messages that changes. If the messages are stored as text files that can easily be edited using any text editor, maintenance should be easy to do. However, it is important to document the help system well so that the association between the help files and the relevant portions of the application program are clear. Ideally, cross-references will appear in both the help system and application program.

For Training/Documentation Specialists

As an ever-increasing number of people come to use computer systems in their daily jobs, more and more training and documentation will take online form. It is simply more convenient and cost effective to provide online training and documentation when everybody has access to the same computer system. The advantages and disadvantages of online and offline documentation are summarized in Table 7–3.

The main advantages of conventional paper documentation are portablity (can be studied/used anywhere), high resolution, and familiarity. The high resolution of print (about 2,000 dots per inch) relative to the low resolution of most display screens (under 300 dots per inch) means that a lot more information can be placed on a page relative to the screen. In fact, this difference in resolution is one factor that accounts for the slower reading speeds of computer displays versus printed pages. (Gould et al., 1987).

The main advantages of online documentation are availability, keyword searching, and ease of distribution. Unlike print documentation which can easily get lost, online documentation is always available when the system is used. One of the significant advantages of online documentation is the ability to search for terms or phrases via keyword searches,—a big improvement over fixed indexing. Another important advantage of online documen-

Table 7-3. Comparison of Online and Offline Documentation

	Advantages	Disadvantages
Offline Documentation	• highly portable • high resolution • familiar	• gets lost • can be bulky • difficult to update
Online Documentation	• always available • keyword searching • easy to distribute	• limited resolution • simultaneous use not always possible

tation is the ease of distributing the documentation—it is provided along with the program itself.

One disadvantage of online documentation is that it is often not possible to study the documentation and the application at the same time. To do this, some form of windowing is needed so that the documentation and application can be on the screen simultaneously.

The last point illustrates the most important consideration about online versus offline documentation. Online documentation has significant advantages over offline documentation provided that these capabilities are used. If they are not, then online documentation is likely to be inferior to conventional documentation. Thus, if online documentation does not provide keyword searching features or is not always updated with new releases of the application program, it is not likely to be an improvement over print documentation. Similarly, if screen resolution is poor or windowing capability is not available, online documentation may be cumbersome and difficult to use, relative to print.

Computer-based training has become a popular training approach (see Gery, 1987; Kearsley, 1983). However conventional methods of using computers for instruction that involve tutorial strategies are largely ineffective in teaching people how to use computers (e.g., Charney & Reder, 1986; Czaja et al., 1986). As discussed in earlier chapters, people tend to adopt a problem-solving (or trial and error) approach to computer learning tasks. The structured format of tutorials is not appropriate for this learning style. Instead, users need a "coach" or "advisor" who can monitor their exploratory behavior and provide guidance when needed.

For this reason, helps are the preferred form of online training for learning how to use computer systems. However, developing a help system powerful enough to carry the full burden of training for a new user is an extremely demanding task. It is more realistic to teach new users in a hands-on lab setting with an instructor present, relying on the helps to deal with typical problems and the instructor to deal with special difficulties.

For Researchers

Chapter 4, as well as other chapters, should provide any researcher with a wealth of ideas for studies on help systems that need to be done. Here are some of the major issues that were covered in Chapter 4:

- What specific features of helps are most important in terms of performance? Looking at the design alternatives discussed in Chapter 2, which alternatives have the most/least impact on the effectiveness of helps?
- What is the best effectiveness measure for helps? Which measure tells us how "helpful" helps are to the user?
- Can a psychological theory of errors be applied to a specific program or computer application and identify what kinds of problems a user will have?
- Can the mental models possessed by users predict their performance and failures using a program and guide the design of effective helps?
- Is it possible to design domain-independent help systems that work across different applications (or must help systems be task dependent)?
- Should helps be designed to accommodate individual differences or can individual differences be accommodated by user-customization capabilities?
- Will the use of natural language interfaces dramatically improve the effectiveness of help systems?
- Do intention-based or goal-directed help systems provide more useful information to users than "dumb" systems?

If help systems are to become a major component of program design, we need a much larger research base to draw on than presently exists. Even though this research may not always have direct application to the design of specific programs, it is useful in uncovering relationships and variables that should be taken into account in design activities.

For the Rest of Us

Most people who read this book are likely to be regular computer users. This means that you should have a healthy self-interest in the effectiveness of help systems. Nobody likes to get stuck in the middle of a program or get the run around from a stupid piece of software. So, here are some questions you should ask about the help system of any program you are thinking of buying or using:

1. Is the help system easy to find and use?
2. Is it easy to return to application after using the help system?
3. Does the help system provide the specific information you need?
4. Can you move around in the help system easily?
5. Can you quit the help system at any time?
6. Are the help messages easy to understand and complete enough?
7. Can you read the help information easily?
8. Can you customize the help system to your preferences?
9. Can you modify the help messages if you desire?
10. Is the help system better than a manual?

If you cannot answer most of these questions positively, you should reject the help system as poorly designed. Although a program could be outstanding even with a poorly designed help system, it would be that much better with a good help system.

Glossary

Bit-map: A type of display in which every picture element (pixel) can be addressed. Contrasts with character-oriented displays in which only predefined characters can be addressed. Bit-mapped displays allow much more detailed text and graphics than character-oriented displays.

Bugs: Errors in programs that prevent them from working as intended.

Bullet proofing: Finding all the errors in a program by means of exhaustive testing.

Cursor: A marker that indicates the location on the screen of the next input. The marker is usually a blinking square, line, or arrow. The cursor can be moved via arrow keys or some kind of pointing device (e.g., mouse, trackball).

Default: An option which is automatically selected if the user does not select or provide an alternative.

Editor: A special type of program that lets you enter and modify text, graphics, sound/speech, or other functions.

File: Information (data) stored on a disk and identified by a unique name for subsequent retrieval.

Function Keys: Special keys provided on the keyboard which have no fixed function. Their function is defined by a program and can be changed as often as desired.

Hardware: The physical components of a computer system (e.g., monitor, disk drives, printers).

Human Factors: The study of human performance, especially in the context of human–machine interaction.

Icons: Visual symbols used to represent options or data (e.g., a symbol of a trash can represents deletion of a file).

Memory Resident Routine: A program that can coexist in memory (RAM) at the same time as another, allowing concurrent (but not simultaneous) operation of both programs. Such programs are sometimes called "desk accessories."

Menu: A list of program options. Can be full screen, a single line, pull-downs, or pull-outs.

(Random Access) Memory (RAM): The part of the computer where programs are stored while being executed. Measured in thousands (K) of bytes.

Mouse: An input device used on many newer computers to move the cursor. The mouse is a small box that can be rolled on a flat surface. The movement of the cursor on the screen matches the movement of the mouse and clicking the button(s) is used to enter a response.

Networking: Multiple computers linked together, usually to share memory, storage, or peripherals (e.g., printers). Can be either local networks (all machines directly connected via cables) or remote networks (using telecommunications).

Overlay: To display one thing on top of another, usually by adding something to the original display.

Operating System: A program which manages the computer and applications programs. Some examples are DOS, CP/M, and Unix(TM).

Paging: New information is shown in separate screens/windows (contrasts with scrolling).

Parser: A program which translates or decodes a symbolic or natural language input sequence.

Pilot Testing: A tryout of a program with actual users.

Pixel: The smallest point that can be addressed on a bit-mapped display screen (abbreviation for picture element).

Program: A set of instructions that makes the computer do something. Programs consist of routines and subroutines. See also *Software*.

Prompt: A message that suggests or requests a user action (e.g., "Save before quiting Y/N?").

Prototype: A sample or demonstration of the actual program to be developed.

RAM (Random Access Memory): See *Memory*.

Real-time: A program that provides immediate (if not instantaneous) response to input. Contrasts with batch programs that must run completely before providing any response to input.

Release: Version of a program that is distributed.

Resolution: The degree of detail that can be displayed on a computer screen, usually measured in pixels per inch.

Scrolling: Information displays continuously (line by line) on the screen. Contrasts with paging, in which new screens replace existing screens entirely. In some operating systems, windows come with scroll bars that allow the user to move the information inside the window horizontally or vertically.

Software: The programs that make a computer do something.

Syntax: The specific structure or form of a command or expression.

Variables: Labels given to values in a program which can change.

Windows: Defining a portion of the screen for display. Overlapping or "pop-up" windows are displayed on top of the current display.

References

Aaronson, A. & Carroll, J.M. Intelligent Help in a One-Shot Dialog: A Protocol Study. *ACM CHI'87 Proceedings*, Toronto, 1987, 163–168.

Aitkenhead, A.M., & Slack, J.M. *Issues in Cognitive Modeling*. Hillsdale, NJ: Erlbaum Assoc., 1986.

Ambardar, A.K. Human Computer Interaction and Individual Differences. In G. Salvendy (Ed.), *Human-Computer Interaction*. New York: Elsevier, 1984, 207–211.

Anderson, J.R. *The Architecture of Cognition*. Cambridge, MA: Harvard University Press, 1983.

Bailey, R. *Human Error in Computer Systems*. Englewood Cliffs: NJ: Prentice-Hall, 1983.

Bannon, L.J. Helping Users Help Each Other. In D. Norman & S. Draper (Eds.), *User Centered System Design*. Hillsdale, NJ: Erlbaum Assoc., 1986.

Borenstein, N.S. *The Design and Evaluation of On-line Help Systems*. Unpublished doctoral dissertation, Carnegie-Mellon University, Pittsburgh, 1985.

Brockmann, J.R. *Writing Better Computer User Documentation*. New York: Wiley, 1986.

Card, S., Moran, T., & Newell, A. *The Psychology of Human-Computer Interaction*. Hillsdale, NJ: Erlbaum Assoc., 1983.

Carroll, J.M. The Adventure of Getting to Know a Computer. *IEEE Computer*, 1982, 15, 49–58.

Carroll, J.M., & Carrithers, C. Training Wheels in a User Interface. *Communications of the ACM*, August 1984, *27(8)*, 800–806.

Carroll, J.M., & Mazur, S.A. LisaLearning. *IEEE Computer*, November 1986, *19(11)*, 35–49.

Charney, D.H. & Reder, C.M. Designing Interactive Tutorials for Computer Users. *Human-Computer Interaction*, 1986, *2*, 297–317.

Cohill, A.M., & Williges, R.C. Retrieval of HELP Information for Novice Users of Interactive Computer Systems. *Human Factors*, 1985, *27(3)*, 335–343.

Conklin, J. Hypertext: An introduction and survey. *IEEE Computer*, 1987, *20(9)*, 17–41.

Czaja, S.J., Hammond, K., Blascovich, J.J., & Swede, H. Learning to Use A Word Processing System as a Function of Training Strategy. *Behavior and Information Technology*, 1986, *5*, 203–216.

Dillon, R.F., & Schmeck, R.R. (Eds.) *Individual Differences in Cognition*. New York: Academic Press, 1985.

Elkerton, J. Online Aiding for Human-Computer Interfaces. In M. Helander (Ed.), *Handbook of Human-Computer Interaction*. Amsterdam: Elsevier, 1987.

Estes, W.K. (Ed.) *Handbook of Learning and Cognitive Processes*. (*Vols. 1–6*). Hillsdale, NJ: Erlbaum Assoc., 1975–1978.

Eysenck, M.W. *A Handbook of Cognitive Psychology*. Hillsdale, NJ: Erlbaum Assoc., 1975.

Finin, T.W. Providing Help and Advice in Task Oriented Systems. *Proceedings of International Joint Conference on Artificial Intelligence (IJCAI)*, Karlsruhe, W. Germany, 1983, 288–294.

Fischer, G., Lemke, A., & Schwab, T. Knowledge-based Help Systems. *ACM CHI'85 Proceedings*, San Francisco, 1985, 161–167.

Gentner, D. & Stevens, L. (Eds.) *Mental Models*. Hillsdale, NJ: Erlbaum Assoc., 1983.

Gery, G. *CBT: Making It Happen*. Boston, MA: Weingarten Publications, 1987.

Gomez, L., Egan, D.E., & Bowers, C. Learning to Use a Text Editor: Some Learner Characteristics that Predict Success. *Human-Computer Interaction, 2(1)*, 1986.

Gould, J.D., Alfaro, L., Finn, R., Haupt, B., Minuto, A., & Salaun, J. Why Reading Was Slower From CRT Displays Than From Paper. *ACM CHI'87 Proceedings*, Toronto, 1987, 7–11.

Houghton, R.C. Online Help Systems: A Conspectus. *Communications of the ACM*, February 1984, *27(2)*, 126–133.

Johnson-Laird, P.N. *Mental Models*. Cambridge, MA: Harvard University Press, 1983.

Judd, W. Beyond the Menu Screen: What a Help System Can Be. *Data Training Magazine*, July 1986a, 24–27.

Judd, W. What, Exactly, Is Your Problem? An Introduction to Dynamic Help. *Data Training Magazine*, August 1986b, 36–37.

Kearsley, G. Computer Based Training: *A Guide to Selection and Implementation*. Reading, MA: Addison-Wesley, 1983.

Kellogg, W.A., & Breen, T.J. Evaluating User and System Models: Applying Scaling Techniques to Problems in Human-Computer Interaction. *ACM CHI'87 Proceedings*, Toronto, 1987, 303–308.

Lehner, P.E., & Zirk, D.A. Cognitive Factors in User/Expert-System Interaction. *Human Factors*, 1987, *29(1)*, 97–109.

Magers, C.S. An Experimental Evaluation of Online HELP for Non-Programmers. *ACM CHI'83 Proceedings*, Boston, 1983, 277–281.

Mark, W. Natural language help in the CONSUL system. *National Computer Conference Proceedings*, 1982, *51*, 475–479.

Norman, D. Design Rules Based On Analyses of Human Error. *Communications of the ACM*, 1983, *4*, 254–258.

O'Malley, C.O., Smolensky, P., Bannon, L., Conway, E., Graham, J., Sokolov, J., & Monty, M.L. A Proposal for User Centered System Documentation. *ACM CHI'83 Proceedings*, Boston, 1983, 282–285.

Relles, N. *The Design and Implementation of User-Oriented Systems*. Unpublished doctoral dissertation, University of Wisconsin, Madison, 1979.

Rich, E.A., & Morgan, H.L. Programs as data for their help systems. *National Computer Conference Proceedings*, 1982, *51*, 481–485.

Rissland, E.L., Valcarce, E.M., & Ashley, K.D. Explaining and Arguing with Examples. *Proceedings of AAAI Conference*, Austin, TX, 1984, 288–294.

Royce, J.R. & Powell, A. *Theory of Personality and Individual Differences: Factors, Systems, and Processes*. Englewood Cliffs, NJ: Prentice-Hall, 1983.

Shneiderman, B. *Designing the User Interface*. Reading, MA: Addison-Wesley, 1987.

Vicente, K., Hayes, B. C., & Williges, R.C. Assaying and Isolating Individual Differences in Searching a Hierarchical File System. *Human Factors*, 1987, *29 (3)*, 349–359.

Walker, J.H. Issues and Strategies for Online Documentation. *IEEE Transactions on Professional Communication*, in press.

Wilensky, R., Arens, Y.,& Chin, D. Talking to UNIX in English: An Overview of UC. *Communications of the ACM*, June 1984, *27 (6)*, 574–593.

Yoder, C.M. *An Expert System for Providing On-Line Information Based Upon Knowledge of Individual User Characteristics*. Unpublished doctoral dissertation, Syracuse University, 1986.

Zemke, R., & Kramlinger, R. *Figuring Things Out*. Reading, MA: Addison-Wesley, 1983.

Appendix A: Programming Considerations

This Appendix discusses programming considerations for some of the design alternatives discussed in Chapter 2.

Static Helps

The simplest kind of static help systems involve searching a help message data file for the term entered or selected from a menu list and displaying the message. The data file would look something like this:

> *$help_1$/this is help message 1.
> *$help_2$/this is help message 2.
> . . . .
> *$help_n$/this is help message n.

The search routine would check each term to see if it matches until it has found a match or exhausted the file.

Searching through the entire file may yield poor response if the file is large. Instead, the terms can be kept in a list and the list is searched. When a match is found, the position in the list is used to index the message data file.

In multi-level helps that allow the user to specify the type of help desired, the records in the help message data file must be designated according to the type of information, e.g.:

```
*help1/example/this is an example for help 1
*help1/format/this is the format for help 1
*help1/exceptions/these are the exceptions for help1
. . . etc.
```

Again, if the data file was large, some sort of indexing scheme should be used to avoid searching the entire file. For example, the data file could be conceptualized as a matrix with each column corresponding to a different type of help. Any message could be found using a two-valued vector: message (help#, type).

The routine for a command entry help system might look like this:

```
If input string= "help" then
      Get next word
      If next word = null
         Then display general help message
      Else If next word = {help1,help2 . . . helpn}
         Then display specific help message
      Else display "help not found" message
Else continue
```

Context Sensitive Helps

The basic mechanism used to provide context sensitivity is a two element vector that specifics the current function and current state, that is:

Get help message (function_n, state_m)

The function specifies the current command that the user is trying to use and the state refers to the location in the program or status. For example, if the user is trying to create a file and receives an invalid filename error, the function = file creation and the state = invalid filename error. A help message data file must be created with entries for every meaningful combination of functions and states.

When the user requests help, the system must identify the current function being used and the current state. This means that a unique identifier must be given to each function/state in the program and be stored in a standard memory location or variable.

Subroutine/procedure names can sometimes be used for this purpose but in many cases the identifiers will be constants (either text strings or numbers) specifically inserted for the help system.

Instead of being sensitive to the current state of the system, the system could be sensitive to the state of the user. Thus, the state element indicates some user dimension such as experience level, personality characteristics or preferences. It is also possible for the vector to have more than two elements. For example a three element vector could be sensitive to current function, current system state, and current user state.

Dialog Helps

A dialog help system works by matching user responses against a script for the task or operation being performed. The script lists each separate action that the user must make and the correct (or alternative) responses in terms of keypresses, menu selections, or cursor movements. Corresponding to each step is a prompt message to be displayed.

The main routine for a dialog help system would look like this:

```
If not last task step then
        Display prompt message for step_n
        Check user response
        If reponse is correct then
                Step_n = next step
            Else display remedial message
Else quit help
```

Note that there might be a number of "correct" responses at any given step, in which case the response must be matched against a number of alternatives. The remedial message usually states that the response made was incorrect and redisplays the prompt message for the current step.

A parser is needed to check the correctness of the response. If the response is a single keypress or "yes/no", a simple string match is involved. On the hand, if the response is a complicated sequence such as a formula or a natural language expression, the parser will need to use some form of tree or list structures to determine if it matches.

The message data file for a dialog type help system will require a different message for each step in the script and each response alternative that can be matched.

One of the important decisions to be made in implementing a dialog type help is the "grain" size of the steps. If the steps are too big (i.e., combine too many substeps), the user may get lost or confused. If the steps are too small, the helps sequence may be too tedious and slow for most users.

Displaying Helps

In most cases, the details of how help messages can be displayed will be largely determined by the operating system software (e.g., the availability and type of windowing possible).

While it possible to directly format the help message data file for display if the windows are fixed in size, this is not a good idea. When the help messages are changed, the formating will need to be redone. Instead, a fomating routine should be written that reads the help message and separates the lines to fit into the display window.

If you are displaying help messages in windows and the help messages are sometimes longer than the window size, you will need a paging or scrolling routine. This routine will keep track of the line count as it displays the help message and stop reading the message file when the last line of the window is reached. When the user selects the next page or scrolls down in the window, reading the file continues until the end of the message is reached or the window is full again. In systems where the user can resize the window, the routine must take into account the current dimensions (and hence line count) of the window.

Extensibility

There are three kinds of extensibility that can be provided in a help system:

- Add a new help term or message
- Delete or change an existing term or message
- Add a synonym or cross-reference for an existing term

Providing an extensible help system has two components: some form of editor that allows the user to perform their addition/change, and help data files that can be modified easily by this editor.

The editor can be a line or screen-oriented editor depending upon the display environment of the computer system involved. In either case, basic editing capabilities such as backspace, character insert/delete, and copy (cut & paste) should be provided. The editor should be designed so that the existing help term or message is shown when an editing operation is started, and the changed term or message shown after an editing operation..

Data files that are organized in the same fashion as are they are presented in the editor will be be easier to program. If extensive rearrangement of the data files is involved or a complex indexing scheme is used, performance may suffer. Obviously, it is desirable to know whether the help system will be extensible when designing the help file structure.

Hypertext

Implementing a hypertext system is relatively easy. All that is required is the ability to identify the screen coordinates of the cursor when a hypertext item is selected. The screen location points to a help message to be displayed or some form of help action. When scrolling is involved, the system must keep track of what is currently being displayed and match the screen coordinates with the correct portion of the file being viewed. A list of the active hypertext items and their current screen coordinates can be kept for each new screen display to speed up searching.

On the other hand, the data files for a hypertext system are usually very complicated. Each item must include a specification of what type of item it is (e.g., glossary item, cross-reference, note) and all links with other items in the data base. Developing and testing all of these specifications is tedious and makes creation of a hypertext system very time consuming.

Appendix B: Software Tools

This Appendix describes an assortment of software tools commercially available for personal computers that could be used in the development of help systems. Similar tools exist (or should) for mainframes, minis, and workstations. These programs are included as illustrative examples and no endorsement is intended.

Bricklin's DEMO Program
(PC/MS DOS)

Software Garden Inc.
Box 373
Newton Highlands, MA 02161
(617) 332-2240

Dan Bricklin is one of the orginal developers of Visicalc and a pioneer in the PC software field. DEMO is a program developed by Bricklin that lets you create sophisticated slide slows very easily and quickly. These slide shows can be used as prototypes for testing out design ideas or collecting user data.

DEMO has many features and includes a capture program that lets you copy screens from other (monochrome) programs and then modify them. This is especially useful for creating help prototypes because you can experiment with different designs using the actual application screens.

DOS-Helper
(PC/MS-DOS)

Aristo Software
16811 El Camino Read, Suite 213
Houston, TX 77058
(713) 480-6288

DOS-Helper provides an online help system for the DOS operating system. The system provides detailed explanations of each DOS command and major concepts. The program can be installed as memory resident. New help messages can be added by the user.

Flash-Up Windows
(PC/MS DOS)

Software Bottling Co. of New York
6600 Long Island Expressway
Maspeth, N.Y. 11378
(718) 458–3700

Flash-Up Windows is a window generator and editor that lets you create "pop-up" windows for any application program. Flash-Up works as a memory resident program and loads windows over top of the current screen when a special "hot key" is pressed (e.g., Alt-Home). The window editor allows the creation of windows from 4×4 to 24×80 characters wide.

The Flash-Up program can be used to created context-sensitive helps by assigning different windows to different functions or parts of the application program. Flash-up also lets you create menus in windows that call other windows. This could be used to create static helps.

Guide
(Macintosh & IBM PC)

Owl International, Inc.
14218 NE 21st St.
Bellevue, WA 98007
(206) 451–2286

Guide is one of the first commercial products available that allows you to create hypertext documents. Using hypertext, a help system can be designed that allows multidimensional links among terms and concepts.

HELP/Control
(PC/MS DOS)

MDS Inc.
Box 1237
Portland, ME 04104
(207) 772–5436

HELP/Control consists of HELP/Runtime subroutines and HELP/Popup, a help screen compiler. The HELP/Runtime subroutines can be inserted in existing programs to provide context-sensitive helps. The subroutines are available for most major programming languages, including C, Pascal, Basic, Fortran, Cobol, and assembly. HELP/Popup provides memory resident access for help screens.

HELP/Control allows a number of different design approaches. Help screens can be created with a built-in screen design language or can be created using Bricklin's DEMO program and then translated. Alternatively, help screens can be created from text files using a formating utility available.

Rescue
(PC/MS DOS)

Polaris Software
613 West Valley Pkwy, Suite 323
Escondido, CA 92025
(619) 743–7800

Another window editor program that lets you create memory resident help screens. Text files can also be used. Provides security feature that allows you to restrict access and modification rights to authorized users.

SIMPLE
(PC/MS DOS)

Software Merchants Unlimited
3767 Overland Ave.
Los Angeles, CA 90034
(213) 837–4456

System IMPLementation by Example (SIMPLE) is an application generator that produces programs from example screens. The program is based upon a relational database framework, has a spreadsheet type interface, and includes a built-in report generator.

The program allows you define your own menus and help/tutorial screens making it useful as a prototying tool (especially for applications that have a database/report generation structure).

Shelley
(PC/MS DOS)

ComTrain, Inc.
152 Mill St.
Grass Valley, CA 95945
(916) 273–0845

Shelley is a concurrent authoring system that lets you build an online reference, help, or tutorial program on top of an existing application program. It provides a range of response processing options.

The Shelly system was used to develop the SHERPA help program discussed in chapter 3.

UserGuide
(Macintosh)

Shana Enterprises Inc.
9704–54 Ave., #200
Edmonton, Alberta
Canada T6E 0A9
(403) 438–6548

UserGuide is an online help tool for the Apple Macintosh. The program allows you to create a user guide (static helps) which can be accessed from any program from the Desk Accessory menu.

Vasco
(PC/MS DOS,
also mainframes, minis)

Vasco Corp.
1919 S.Highland Ave., #118
Lombard, IL 60148
(312) 495–0755

Vasco offers a number of concurrent authoring programs that let you build online glossaries, helps, or tutorial programs on top of an existing application program.

AUTHOR INDEX

A
Aaronson, A., 57, *97*
Aitkenhead, A.M., 50, *97*
Alfaro, L., 89, *98*
Ambardar, A.K., 54, *97*
Anderson, J.R., 4, 50, 51, *97*
Arens, Y., 59, *99*
Ashley, K.D., 57, *99*

B
Bailey, R., 51, *97*
Bannon, L.J., 18, 25, *97, 99*
Blascovich, J.J., 90, *98*
Borenstein, N.S., 47, *97*
Bowers, C., 55, *98*
Breen, T.J., 53, *98*
Brockmann, J.R., 10, *97*

C
Card, S., 4, 51, 56, *97*
Carrithers, C., 52, 53, *97*
Carroll, J.M., 52, 53, 57, *97*
Charney, D.H., 90, *97*
Chin, D., 59, *99*
Cohill, A.M., 46, 47, *97*
Conklin, J., 19, *98*
Conway, E., 18, *99*
Czaja, S.J., 90, *98*

D
Dillon, R.F., 54, *98*

E
Egan, D.E., 55, *98*
Elkerton, J., 51, *98*
Estes, W.K., 50, *98*
Eysenck, M.W., 50, *98*

F
Finin, T.W., 56, *98*
Finn, R., 89, *98*
Fischer, G., 57, *98*

G
Gentner, D., 53, *98*
Gery, G., 90, *98*
Gomez, L., 55, *98*
Gould, J.D., 89, *98*
Graham, J., 18, *99*

H
Hammond, K., 90, *98*
Haupt, B., 89, *98*
Hayes, B.C., 55, *89*
Houghton, R.C., 49, *98*

J
Johnson-Laird, P.N., 53, *98*
Judd, W., 10, 16, *98*

K
Kearsley, G., 90, *98*
Kellogg, W.A., 53, *98*
Kramlinger, R., 64, *99*

L
Lehner, P.E., 53, *98*
Lemke, A., 57, *98*

M
Magers, C.S., 48, *98*
Mark, W., 56, *98*
Mazur, S.A., 52, *97*
Minuto, A., 89, *98*
Monty, M.L., 18, *99*
Moran, T., 4, 51, 56, *97*
Morgan, H.L., 57, *99*

N
Newell, A., 4, 51, 56, *97*
Norman, D., 51, *99*

O
O'Malley, C.D., 18, *99*

P
Powell, A., 54, *99*

R
Reder, C.M., 90, *97*
Relles, N., 46, *99*
Rich, E.A., 57, *99*
Rissland, E.L., 56, *99*
Royce, J.R., 54, *99*

S
Salaun, J., 89, *98*
Schmeck, R.R., 54, *98*
Schwab, T., 57, *98*
Shneiderman, B., 4, 49, *99*
Slack, J.M., 50, *97*
Smolensky, P., 18, *99*
Sokolov, J., 18, *99*
Stevens, L., 53, *98*
Swede, H., 90, *98*

V
Valarce, E.M., 56, *99*
Vicente, K., 55, *99*

W
Walker, J.H., 10, *99*
Wilensky, R., 59, *99*
Williges, R.C., 46, 47, 55, *97*, *99*

Y
Yoder, C.M., 54, *99*

Z
Zemke, R., 64, *99*
Zirk, D.A., 53, *98*

SUBJECT INDEX

A
ACT*, 51
Age, 55
Artificial intelligence, 7, 56–59
ASCII, 24
Associative networks, 17
Authoring tools, 66

B
Band aids, 82
Bookmarking, 25
Bullet proofing, 67–68
Bulletin boards, 25

C
Checkbook balancing, 54
Cognitive psychology, 7, 51
Cognitive style, 54
Comment routine, 78–79
Computer experience, 80
Computer-based training, 89
Concurrent, 3
Confidence, 46
Configuration, 23
Constraints, 25
Content, 3
Context sensitivity, 15, 31, 33, 56
Cross-references, 89
CROSSTALK, 28

D
Data collection, 72, 78
Data entry, 29
Debugging program, 38
Decisions about design, 72, 87
Development schedules, 69
Dialog, 16
Documentation, 9, 38, 89
DOS, 52
DP/MIS managers, 86

E
Electronic mail, 25, 31
Error-handling, 3
Errors, 52–53
Experience, 4

F
Field dependence, 54
File manipulation, 48
File searching, 55
File structure, 24
Financial benefits, 71
Function keys, 19

G
GOMS, 51
GUIDE, 41

H
Hierarchical, 35
Human advisors, 57
Human factors, 10
Hypertext, 19

I
Implementation cycle, 62
Individual differences, 2, 54–56
Interface, 3
Interruption, 9

K
Knowledge-based, 57

L
Labor costs, 71
Large-scale systems, 25
Learning curve, 71
LISP, 37
LOTUS, 33

M
Maintenance, 84, 87
Marketing costs, 70
MCI MAIL, 31
MELVYL, 40
Mental models, 53
Menu, 18
Mistakes, 51
Models, 6
Mouse, 38
Myers-Brigg, 54

N
Networks, 25, 31

O
Operating system, 29, 52, 54
Optimization, 20

P
Parser, 18
Payoffs, 69
Personality characteristics, 2
Preemptive, 52
Print capability, 24
Problems, 76
Product support, 71
Program integrity, 23
Programmers, 37
Programming implications, 23
Proofing, 67
Protocol analysis, 52
Pull-down menus, 19

Q
Quality, 8
Quality-control, 79
Questionnaires, 67, 79

R
RAM, 25
Readability, 55
Real-time systems, 87
Release, 68
Response time, 25
Responsiveness, 9

S
Safety net, 3
Scheduling, 86
Screen management, 20
Scroll-bar, 22
SHERPA, 35–36
Skills, 87
Spatial ability, 55
Speed, 25
SYMBOLICS, 37
Synonyms, 23
Syntax, 28
Syntax errors, 18

T
Task completion time, 49
Telephone hotline, 31
Terminals, 25
Text editing, 46, 56
Theory, 7
Training, 9, 89
Training wheels, 53

U
UNIX, 18, 47, 59
Usability, 3
User
  behavior, 4
  errors, 52
  experience, 80, 87
  models, 56
  response data, 67
  tryouts, 86

V
VAX/VMX, 48
VM, 29, 54
VM SCHEDULE, 29

W
Windows, 21, 76
WORDSTAR, 30

Tolley's Tax Computations 2017/18

by

Kevin Walton MA

David Smailes FCA

Tolley®

Members of the LexisNexis Group worldwide

United Kingdom	RELX (UK) Limited, trading as LexisNexis, Lexis House, 30 Farringdon Street, London EC4A 4HH
Australia	LexisNexis Butterworths, Chatswood, New South Wales
Austria	LexisNexis Verlag ARD Orac GmbH & Co KG, Vienna
Benelux	LexisNexis Benelux, Amsterdam
Canada	LexisNexis Canada, Markham, Ontario
China	LexisNexis China, Beijing and Shanghai
France	LexisNexis SA, Paris
Germany	LexisNexis Deutschland GmbH, Munster
Hong Kong	LexisNexis Hong Kong, Hong Kong
India	LexisNexis India, New Delhi
Italy	Giuffrè Editore, Milan
Japan	LexisNexis Japan, Tokyo
Malaysia	Malayan Law Journal Sdn Bhd, Kuala Lumpur
New Zealand	LexisNexis NZ Ltd, Wellington
Singapore	LexisNexis Singapore, Singapore
South Africa	LexisNexis Butterworths, Durban
USA	LexisNexis, Dayton, Ohio

First Published in 1987

Published by LexisNexis

A CIP Catalogue record for this book is available from the British Library.

ISBN for this volume: 9780754553878

Printed and bound by Hobbs the Printers Ltd, Totton, Hampshire

Visit LexisNexis at www.lexisnexis.co.uk